Reversal Trading

2022

The Best Reversal Strategies

In less than 5 days

TABLE OF CONTENTS

INTRODUCTION

Like any other endeavor, good trading should be simple. In other words, you shouldn't employ too many systems or indicators at the same time. But, success in financial trading goes hand-in-hand with good organizational skills.

Frequently, traders fail to organize their trades by neglecting to put their system into the bigger picture of the market. This may lead to more unexpected losses, which will affect their trading beliefs and attitudes. Once they lose the necessary positive attitude in trading, things will be much harder as they go forward.

Think about it... You must optimize everything in your life, from basic skills, like how to speak, how to listen, how to negotiate with others, etc. We are taught to implement things in a way that generates the best possible results. However, the fact is that we cannot perform well until lots of effort has been made. We learn from mistakes, understanding which attempts can be improved and which should be retained to achieve better results while suiting our style. In short, we need to optimize strategies, techniques, and tips via "trial and error" to find a way to sustainable success.

Things are exactly the same in trading. Although many "profitable" strategies and patterns have existed for a long time, not everyone makes good use of them. As a matter of fact, not understanding enough about market momentum behind the candlesticks patterns costs traders a lot of hard-earned money. In this book, you will see how I identify these momentums using pure price actions. The reversal trading techniques presented in the book may help you make some BIG steps on the way to consistent profits in trading. They are proven methods that I have been using consistently for years, which would save you a lot of time unlocking trading mysteries. Yet, it will not free you from necessary back-tests via your trading platform, which will help you get a deeper understanding of the new concepts I am conveying. Most importantly, you need to be patient, sticking to secrets on **market structures** and the **3MS principle** for a long enough time. Bear in mind that all good things in life take time, and success in trading is not an exception.

Also, keep in mind that while many of the real examples in the book are from the currency market, the concepts apply well in any other markets.

Now, let's get started.

CHAPTER I: PRICE ACTION TRADING

Price action is the core of the trading strategies presented in this book. Therefore, let's first take a brief look at this popular concept. I believe that after reading and grasping what I convey about reversal trading in this book, you will have a much deeper understanding of price action. All strategies and techniques I present in this book help answer the question: What is price action?

Price action describes some characteristics of an asset's price movements, which are normally analyzed in connection with price fluctuations in the recent past. Put simply, price action is a trading style that enables traders to read market signals and make trading decisions based on recent historical data, instead of relying wholly on complex technical indicators.

This trading style takes many technical analysis tools into account, including but not limited to charts, support/resistance, trend lines, price ranges, swing highs and swing lows. Which tools to use depends on each trader's preference, but a price action trader generally keeps the chart simple. The trader would believe the most important source of analysis data comes from the price and the candlesticks, and everything else is built upon these two elements. For example, if the market is creating higher highs and higher lows, it tells the price action trader that an uptrend is in place. The trader then assesses, based on the aggressiveness of the buyers, whether the trend is likely to continue before identifying a trade setup and trigger.

Compared to technical indicators, price action can free traders from complex formulas and time-consuming analysis. Although technical indicators use price as their basis, they often lag behind the price, meaning they often provide belated data for analysis. By simply focusing on the price, traders get the information in real-time instead of waiting for a lagging signal that might mislead their trading decision.

As a price action trader, you should be patient, waiting for opportunities to come and analyzing them based on price action signals, ideally in conjunction with some popular patterns such as trend lines, break-outs, channels, etc. Trading setups based on price action analysis don't appear very often, but once they are present on the chart, chances are that they are well worth careful monitoring and analyzing.

Candlestick patterns such as the pin bar, engulfing pattern, and double top/bottom are typical examples of visually-interpreted price action formations. There are more candlestick formations that are generated from price actions to project what may come next in the chart. In this book, we will focus on these three patterns with in-depth analysis. From a new and interesting angle, we will explore the insights into fatal mistakes traders often make in trading.

In the next chapter, let's discuss some crucial philosophies that differentiate successful traders from losers in the markets.

CHAPTER II: SHAPE YOUR MINDSET FOR SUCCESS IN TRADING

As you might have heard, trading psychology accounts for around 60% of traders' success in trading. Hence, before employing any trading systems or strategies, it is important you understand the importance of an appropriate mindset in trading and how it should become second nature to you. Without a correct understanding of the way the market operates, what the opportunities and dangers are, you will be overwhelmed by a lot of market signals, causing an imbalanced state of mind, where loss is inevitable.

Below are some of the most basic yet important characteristics of trading:

The unpredictability of the market

If you have certain experience in trading, you would agree with me that the market is just unpredictable. In its purest form, the market is the reflection of what all traders all over the world think and act. Meanwhile, candlestick charts are the visualization of the overall market momentum which traders use to analyze possible market movements.

In fact, it is nearly impossible to tell with certainty where the market is going next. There are so many institutions, banks, funds, and individual traders participating in the market every day. Each entity has its own thoughts and courses of action. You might think this price is high and that price is low, however, others may think and act oppositely. You cannot know what others are thinking about the same candlestick patterns you are watching. Also, you cannot affect others in a way that they will follow your thinking and trading preferences. As a matter of fact, each time in the market is unique and nothing is known for sure.

Basically, trading in its purest form is a field of probabilities. If you join each trade with a high probability of stacking the odds in your favor, you are likely to win in the long term (this book will focus on how you can obtain such *a high probability*).

Throughout my trading career, I have seen many traders suffer from negative feelings after some losing trades. Yet, we must keep in mind that we cannot avoid losses all the time. Even the most successful traders in the world suffer from losses, and sometimes the losses are high, to be frank. The key is how you manage your losses within a safe and acceptable zone, in a way that they cannot affect your psychological state of mind and your overall profitability picture. Consistently profitable traders are well aware of this, and they never violate their rules on money management, which gives them an appropriate frame of mind to join the market.

I want to emphasize the unpredictability of the market because I fully understand how stressed most traders are when they experience losses. Successful traders never let these losses undermine and drive them to self-sabotaging actions. For them, the market is unpredictable, and the core elements in any success in trading lie in their own thoughts and beliefs. Specifically, if one is loyal to appropriate trading rules and philosophy, they can eventually make consistent profits.

This is also my first advice when it comes to trading in any market. When you are in an environment with lots of uncertainties, the adoption of a proper mindset is a MUST. One single loss or even a number of losses will not tell you anything about your analysis and your system. In fact, the best systems still generate many losing trades. It is how you remain disciplined and objective in the market that matters most. Strict compliance with rules will help to free you from unexpected pains resulting from losses. The better you are at avoiding psychological shocks, the better you are at identifying opportunities via candlesticks. While the market is full of unpredictability, it offers unlimited chances for making profits. The concern here is whether you are willing and committed to doing the right things to acquire desired results.

Trading should be flexible

After all, trading should be flexible. This means that you should let your mind be open to movements in the market. Sometimes, candlesticks move according to your analysis and expectations, but in many other cases, their movements make you puzzled. As I mentioned above, the market is comprised of a large number of participants and you cannot know what others are thinking. A price level you consider high may be seen as low in others' eyes. To achieve success in this endeavor, you need to accept the "uncertainty characteristic" of the market.

When you are flexible, you can analyze charts based on what the market is actually telling you, instead of what you feel or hope. Flexibility puts you in the best position to discover potential opportunities when they come. Moreover, this also serves to free you from negative feelings or psychological shocks when things go against your expectations. This is different from a rigid style, in which you rely too much or put too much expectation on any single trade setup or trigger.

Let's take a hypothetical example of a trader who is seeing a "seemingly" similar pattern on the chart to one that he successfully traded a few months earlier. I use the word "seemingly" because I cannot ensure everything behind the candlesticks is identical to the situation in which he traded before. In fact, the "similar pattern" is just on the surface. However, he is completely confident that the history will repeat, and places a trade with a high volume. The market then generates some initial signs of opposition movements to what he had thought, but he ignores it and continues with his original analysis. He criticizes any opposing ideas on the belief that if he could win once with this setup, he can win many more times. He considers anyone who is not in favor of his trade as silly because he is "experienced" in trading this candlestick pattern. He becomes overconfident and cannot grasp what the market really wants to tell him. Finally, he ends up losing a big unexpected amount of money that is far beyond his imagination.

I bet this scenario isn't strange to most traders. These unexpected losses greatly contribute to wiping out traders' accounts regardless of which assets or instruments they are trading. In the example above, our trader is lacking an objective mindset to pick up what is happening in the market. In other words, he is not flexible enough to understand a fact that each moment in the market is unique, and directly copying previous actions may lead to disaster. Only by staying calm, open-minded, and flexible can someone be able to uncover the potential opportunities the market offers.

This is what I want to convey in relation to the analysis techniques that you will discover in the following chapters of this book. In fact, these techniques are the result of a large amount of time I spent in front of my computer screen studying, trading, and summarizing. Yet, I do not guarantee these techniques will work each time you trade with them. I am just confident that if you apply them consistently, you will be profitable in the long term. Always be open-minded and listen to what the candlesticks want to tell you. In trading, flexibility is a MUST.

The role of identifying the correlation between bulls and bears

The market is characterized by the battle between buyers and sellers, or bulls and bears. Each candle on the chart illustrates the correlation between the two sides. For example, if the bears are more powerful than the bulls, the market is showing a downtrend, forming lower highs and lower lows, and vice versa. On the other hand, if the bears are tired, the market may fail to create lower highs and lower lows.

During those times, traders should watch out for signals from the bulls participating in the market. It sounds simple, but it is a BIG key in determining whether or not we should buy or at least be in a position for a buy order. If the market is telling us that sellers are losing steam and buyers are gaining strength, start looking for a long setup. Failing to do that means that you are missing a chance, or worse, losing money in the market.

Furthermore, the identification of the dominant side should be based on the big picture. One single candlestick does not count in many cases. The big picture should include but not be limited to an overall trend determined on both longer and shorter timeframes, support/resistance, and trend lines. Later in this book, I will describe in more detail when the sellers and buyers are tired, and what we should do in those times. Successful trading in the financial market is closely aligned with analyzing the correlation between buyers and sellers. It can only be done by analyzing the charts yourself. No robot can replace a human to do this task.

After understanding the big picture, you will start looking for high probability trade setups in the market and then find an entry price, stop-loss, and profit-taking level. While the battle between bulls and bears never ends, each correction or retracement in the price might often be ideal to place a trade. For example, if the bears are dominating the market, any correction created from the bulls is ideal for placing an entry, and vice versa. In reality, I rarely enter any trade without correction (also referred to as a retest), except for some highly volatile markets such as cryptocurrency. This not only helps me reap greater profits but also allows me to acquire a better risk/reward ratio and cultivate patience.

CHAPTER III: EVERYTHING STARTS WITH THE WAY YOU THINK

How you think is important in order to be a successful trader. Without a proper mindset, it is nearly impossible for you to succeed in a challenging endeavor like trading. Hence, before going deeper into my secret techniques, let's talk about thoughts in trading.

In trading, I divide thoughts into two types:

- **Correct thoughts** may generate correct courses of action, which may result in favorable results.
- **Wrong thoughts** may lead to wrong courses of action, which brings about unexpected results.

In trading, correct thoughts help you generate overall profits through time, while wrong thoughts are the No.1 reason for losses, simple as that. Honestly, I have not witnessed anyone who maintains a wrong mindset and makes consistent profits from the market.

WRONG THOUGHTS AND ACTIONS

Let's discuss the wrong mindsets first.

What is preventing traders from making profits? Remember the moment you decided to join the trading journey. What were the top reasons you decided to open a real trading account at that time? Did you study the market long enough (i.e at least 6 months) and felt so attracted that you opened an account and followed your new passion? Honestly, I don't deny the fact that some traders join the trading journey for good reasons like discovering themselves, studying market secrets that inherently entails lots of practice and patience, acquiring a feeling of conquering, or just simply learning about something new. In my opinion, these are positive reasons to get started. However, many traders join the market for another reason – MONEY. The majority of traders join the market with "profits" as the TOP reason, and that is the problem.

Many traders believe that trading is a simple, quick way to make money. In fact, money can be earned within minutes or even seconds, and there is a lot of money out there. If truth be told, I do not see any other endeavor where people can increase their account balances by just a few mouse clicks, like trading can do. As a matter of fact, the attractiveness of trading is so big that sometimes it may not be possible to say "no" to invitations from brokers or some of your friends. These newbies are seduced by Introducing Brokers (IB) who constantly show off their winning trades. Many traders join with the hope of doubling their account balance in just one or two months, or even less. They dream about financial freedom in which they can make money anywhere in the world with only a laptop connected to the internet. The very thought of money and profits is what I define as a "wrong thought". Trading would be so difficult then.

So, what are the possible wrong actions that may result from this wrong thinking?

- You only focus on profits and don't care about possible losses. You don't accept losses and don't set any stop-loss for your trades. When encountering a floating losing trade, you often hope that on a beautiful day, the market will make a reversal and go favorably.

- You open more trades when you are already in a losing position. For example, if you have a rigid belief that the market will make a reversal, you will sooner or later add another buy order, although the market is moving lower and lower. To make matters worse, you just cannot identify how much profit is acceptable in each trade. You often talk to yourself with some form of "the more, the better".

  Note that the mere addition of trades itself is not a bad act. In fact, it is one of the secrets of maximizing your profits when it's understood and applied appropriately. However, adding another trade arbitrarily is among the quickest ways to wipe out your account. In some cases, you may be right and turn losses into profits. However, sooner or later you will encounter unexpected results from the full focus on your profits.

- You will take revenge against the market. Let's see if this scenario is familiar to you: You are entering a buy trade but the market is trading lower and lower. After adding some buy orders to make up for the first one (in case of a potential reversal), the market is still in a strong downtrend with long bearish candlesticks. There may come a time when you lose hope about a reversal. Then, you enter a higher volume sell order with revenge on your mind, like: *I will get all the losing money back with this trade*. You have very high expectations with this trade. Unfortunately, the bears are "getting tired" of pulling prices lower and start taking profits, which serves to push the price higher. You panic and see your account equity moving closer and closer to the zero level. You cannot do anything else but close your remaining sell order. Your day ends with an overwhelming red color showing lost amounts in your trading history.

- You constantly jump from one trading strategy to another. All you need is a trading strategy that can generate profits consistently. If it fails a few times, you move to another. In this way, any strategy in you use can hardly exist for more than a few months or even weeks. Consequently, you may find yourself using dozens of strategies while you're unsure which work and which don't. In short, failing to consistently follow a trading method long enough could lead to many arbitrary actions where your trading decisions are based on what you *feel* instead of what you *see*.

- Worse, feeling that you cannot win at trading by yourself, you may look for a robot. Robots in trading are advertised by many lousy blogs or sales pages with very high rates of winning. If you still believe in robots, ask yourself this question: "if trading using robots can bring consistent profits, why do 95% of traders lose?". If there is one robot that can turn losers into winners, everyone would be celebrating their victories each day.

- Finally, when you have tried everything possible to help build your account without success, you QUIT. Your mind will then be ingrained into some thoughts like "success in trading is impossible", or "success in trading needs secrets that successful traders never tell you". Your frustration comes to a peak and you become really afraid of entering any trades. Giving up is unavoidable. To make matters worse, because it is a financial failure, it may lead to other unexpected problems between you and your family, your co-investors, your money borrowers, etc. At that time, it is highly likely that you hear a comment like "trading is gambling" from people around you.

An obstacle that prevents you from realizing your mistake is your psychological breakdown. After enduring too many losing trades, you are totally numb toward the market and can't discover any weaknesses to fix. Failure in trading all boils down to wrong thoughts.

CORRECT THOUGHTS AND ACTIONS

From my personal experience, success in trading mainly lies in good money management. You should and must focus on how to **PROTECT YOUR CAPITAL** before thinking of anything else. In other words, *instead of finding a system that brings you winning trades, you should find systems that save you from losing money.* In the last chapter of the book, I will show you the 7-step formula to best protect your trading account and the deep reasons behind these secrets.

Imagine you have just made $100 in the market. If you are too concentrated on profits, you will try to multiply this number as soon as possible. However, as I mentioned above, this thought just serves to ruin your account sooner or later. On the other hand, when you focus on protecting your capital, you are protecting your profits as well, and you stand a good chance of becoming profitable. It's as simple as that. No matter how right or wrong the market is, you have to own a right mindset first, which generates correct actions, specifically:

- Optimize the entry, stop-loss, and profit-taking levels. You will find that optimizing these levels is not an easy task, but it's crucial. The market is not about entering an order when an engulfing pattern or pin bar appears. It is how well you communicate with the market to understand what it is telling you. Sometimes the market is waving at you **"hey, this pin bar is a reliable signal, buy the EUR/USD pair now"**, but in many cases, they are just false/unreliable signals. Hence, to protect your capital, you have to spend more time studying the market and organizing your trades in a better way.

- Concentrate on the risk/reward ratio. The market is a game of probabilities. It is not important if you win or lose in any individual trade. It is important how much you earn when you win and how much you lose when your trade hits the stop-loss level. This also emphasizes the importance of the risk/reward ratio. More on that in the next chapter.

- Use longer timeframes (monthly, weekly, daily, 4-hour charts). In my opinion, these timeframes offer more reliable signals than shorter ones. Moreover, you will realize that in trading, LESS IS MORE. Some newbies may believe that the more trades they enter, the more profits they will gain. However, the truth is the opposite. You must keep in mind that good setups *do not appear very often in the market*. Hence, entering so many trades just serves to take you to various inherent traps in the market, and losses are inevitable. In the next chapter, I will show you an example of how you can avoid this type of trap with a longer timeframe.

- Build a market scenario. Trading patterns tend to repeat in some ways. Studying chart history will give you more insights into the market. From that you can apply patterns and movements into future projections. To win in financial markets, you must be well-organized. In fact, one of the best ways to approach a trade execution is to build a potential scenario for the price movements. If the market continues its movements with your expected analysis, then trade the market based on what you have pre-defined. If not, just stay on the sideline. One thing to remember is the market is always full of opportunities. Stay patient!

In short, if you are losing without understanding the reasons, ask yourself whether you are too concentrated on profits. It is the primary reason traders are constantly wiping out their accounts. If you are focusing on profits, try to pull yourself out of thinking this way. Instead, protecting your hard-earned money should be your top priority.

CHAPTER IV: PRICE ACTION CANNOT WORK WITHOUT THESE THINGS

Besides preparing an appropriate mindset in trading, setting up an effective trading system is imperative to your trading success. Below are some tips that can help you build a profitable trading system. They have been part of my trading for years.

In the following chapters, you will see how I describe my powerful trading strategies in close combination with these elements.

Tip No. 1: Longer timeframes

Choosing an appropriate timeframe to trade depends on each trader's personality. A hungry trade may prefer using shorter ones while a calm-seeking trader tends to seek longer ones (like the daily or weekly charts) and remain in her position longer. Yet, even if you're in favor of fast action, here are some big benefits that you can enjoy using a longer analysis timeframe.

Avoid over-trading: Trading in a short timeframe involves opening and closing trades very quickly. While I am not opposed to this trading style, there are two big dangers you may encounter: over-trading and emotional imbalance. You won't reap a huge profit by using the 15-minute or 30-minute chart to enter and exit your trade. As a result, you add more and more trades, which is, in turn, the No. 1 reason for some detrimental emotions to emerge and destroy your rational thinking. In contrast, by analyzing in a longer frame like the daily or weekly chart (at least the 4-hour chart), it's harder to identify a good trade setup. You'll have to wait for hours or even days to find a true opportunity in the markets, which serves to cultivate your patience as well. This helps you avoid over-trading, emotional trading, arbitrary trading, and helps protect your account. By opting for the very best trade setups, you put the odds more in your favor.

Little noise: When trading short-term moves, traders can easily be affected by sporadic actions from Big Hands in the market. A large enough order can undermine your trade analysis quite easily. In contrast, using a long frame filters out most of the turbulences in the market, paving the way for more reliable trade setups.

Even if you are new to trading and aren't fully aware of over-trading or market noise, thinking of trading as a relationship between individuals will give you a better understanding of longer timeframe trading.

Do you agree that the longer you are with someone, the more you will know about her/him? When you meet someone for the first time, it seems impossible to have a good sense of his or her character within the first 5 minutes of talking. Understandably, you won't be able to have any deep insights one way or another about a person until you spend enough time with him/her. Things are similar in choosing timeframes to trade.

Among the frames mentioned above, the daily chart is the central timeframe in my trading. In this book, you will see that many trade setups or triggers are connected with the daily chart in some ways. We will come back to the daily chart in the last (and very interesting) chapter about capital management and protection.

Now, let's review an example to have a better illustration.

In the 30-minute GBP/USD chart below, can you tell whether the market is in an uptrend or a downtrend?

GBP/USD
30-min chart

It's really hard to tell exactly whether the trend is bullish or bearish, isn't it?

Next, let's compare the 30-minute chart with the daily chart.

From the chart below, even a 6-year-old can see an obvious downtrend. Looking at the daily chart, you could at least determine that you shouldn't buy the currency pair at the current rate. The trend is so strong and there has been no sign of tiredness from the bears. This is how a long timeframe saves you from unexpected losses resulting from the failure to grasp the big picture of the market.

GBP/USD
Daily chart

Jul	Aug	Sep	Oct

1.42000
1.41000
1.40000
1.39000
1.38000
1.37000
1.36400
1.35843
1.35200
1.34600
1.34050

In the next chapters, you will frequently hear about the concept of key support/resistance or key levels. In those cases, you should understand that they are key levels on **longer timeframes** (i.e weekly, daily, or at least the 4-hour chart).

Tip No. 2: An ideal risk/reward ratio (R/R ratio)

As I mentioned, the market is full of uncertainties and no strategy can ensure a high win rate each and every single time you trade. Now, when we talk about success in trading, we are referring to long-term success, aren't we? In fact, when it comes to long-term success, we must think of factors that the more we apply, the more benefits we can enjoy. From my experience, a good risk/reward ratio is one of those factors.

Why risk/reward ratios?

Simply put, we can choose an ideal risk/reward ratio for each trade we take. While ensuring a winning trade is next to impossible, taking a trade with a pre-set R/R ratio is absolutely executable. Put differently, no other forces, from the market to the brokers or traders, can prevent you from choosing a better reward for each risked loss.

Let's say that for each trade, you risk just $1 (limit the loss to just $1) for every $3 of potential profit. In this way, the risk/reward ratio is 1:3. In each trade, what you possibly achieve is three times bigger than what you possibly lose. Hence, if you trade for a long enough period of time, you can lose 75% of all your trades and still won't lose overall, supposing that you risk a similar amount for each trade. This is not to mention that you are using a mediocre trading system (losing 75% of total trades).

Coming back to the above-mentioned ideal ratio, what I mean by "ideal" is at least 1:2.5. In fact, it is even better if it is 1:3, 1:4,1:5, or more. However, finding a trade with a ratio of 1:5 is much harder than finding one with a 1:2.5 rate. On the other hand, I don't object to using the 1:1.5 or 1:2 ratios. Yet, my favorite ratio is at least 1:2.5, which I believe is worth our time waiting, scanning, analyzing, and finally executing trades.

With an ideal R/R ratio, strict money management, and a good trading system, you would be closer to long-term profitability. You won't be too upset when encountering a loss because you are fully aware that losing trades are unavoidable in the market. With a 1:3 ratio, for example, after you win a trade, it will take at least 4 losing trades to cause you to lose overall. Thinking this way, you can relax after each loss. Nothing makes you happier than a belief that you will be profitable eventually.

Tip No. 3: Support/Resistance

In trading, any candlestick pattern must be considered in connection with support/resistance areas. Put differently, I never trade any pattern unless it is present in a support/resistance area.

While the market is full of uncertainties, it often remembers what happened in the past and tends to respect history in some ways. For example, if the 1.2000 level of the EUR/USD pair is represented by a top in the past (from this top, the price wildly fluctuates), the market tends to react when the price touches this level again. It may either bounce back after touching the level or break it and revisit the level (which has now become a support level) at some time in the future.

When the price is about to touch a level, you should watch out for any potential candlestick pattern or chart pattern because these patterns are offering a higher probability of winning than ones not presented on any key levels. Trading this way, we are able to filter out a number of false patterns in the chart.

From my experience, patterns not present on any key levels are often false signals which may cause a disastrous outcome. They might be an indication that the dominant side is recharging its energy and a correction is occurring, but then the prevailing trend strongly continues. Even though some of these patterns may work and the market reverses for some time, it is better to stay on the sideline. In fact, there are unlimited opportunities in the market, and missing out on one or two opportunities should not be treated as a bad thing. From now on, you need to treat trading on key support/resistance your second nature. It is the secret of all successful traders in the world. The more you comply with this rule, the better you will be at filtering out false signals and increasing the probability of success.

Tip No. 4: Risk Per Trade

Maintaining a good risk/reward ratio in each of your trades is not enough if you increase your risk amount arbitrarily.

You may have heard about the 2% rule. The main idea is you shouldn't risk more than 2% of your trading capital in each trade.

For example, if your trading equity is $5,000, you must not risk more than $100 in each trade.

If you want to risk more, increase your trading capital. It may seem difficult for traders to follow, but it is what you should and must do. Trading is a long-term journey, not overnight prosperity.

Good risk management helps you on this journey. As we've said before, the No.1 priority in trading is capital preservation. The No.2 rule is "never forget the No.1 priority".

In fact, the 2% risk amount is still high in my opinion. It's more suitable for seasoned traders who are good at controlling their emotions and managing their trades. For new traders, a risk percentage from 1% to 1.5% is recommended. We'll learn more about that in the last chapter of the book.

Now, let's look at a hypothetical example to see how overly high expectations coupled with selecting an arbitrary trade size could put you in a difficult situation.

Let's say you are spotting a seemingly perfect trade setup on the chart. You did win with a similar setup a few weeks ago. You are confident that history will repeat. You decide to risk five times as much as it should be, and a trade is opened.

Unfortunately, the price goes against your expectation, hitting your stop-loss. You are shocked.

Your over-expectation, coupled with a violation in risk management, costs you your hard-earned money. Now, the stress of looking for a winning trade to make up for that loss is quite big. You may not be as comfortable finding a trade set-up as you were before. Such a circumstance is an ideal condition for some negative feelings to appear such as revenge, stress, depression. This is considered the most dangerous domino effect in financial trading.

In short, for each trader, the risk per trade should be taken into consideration in each trade. Just one violation may cost you not only money but a lot of time to rebuild what you had before. To make matters worse, the re-building process may not be as comfortable as before. This is the problem.

Before discovering the main part of the book, I would like to share with you a little treasure of mine – trading books, notes, and templates and indicator plugins which I believe you would be interested in. Visit https://bit.ly/3zII1Tx for free download.

CHAPTER V: LET'S DEFINE THE TRENDS CORRECTLY

Determining the trends correctly helps avoid false signals. It is well connected with understanding the market momentum, such as whether the bulls or the bears are gaining an advantage. You should not think of buying an asset or instrument when the market is in a strong downtrend, and vice versa. Determining the trend incorrectly is the No.1 reason losses occur.

The trend determination method I apply below is a popular method that can be displayed on a plain chart (i.e., no indicators required). In other words, it is very easy to use. If you have read some popular books on trading, you would agree that the simpler, the better. Hence, all I convey in this book is what I consider simple but effective tips and techniques that I have summarized from my trading journey.

In trading, there are two types of market: trending market and non-trending market.

1. Trending market

A trending market can be either an uptrend or a downtrend. Let's take a look at the example below:

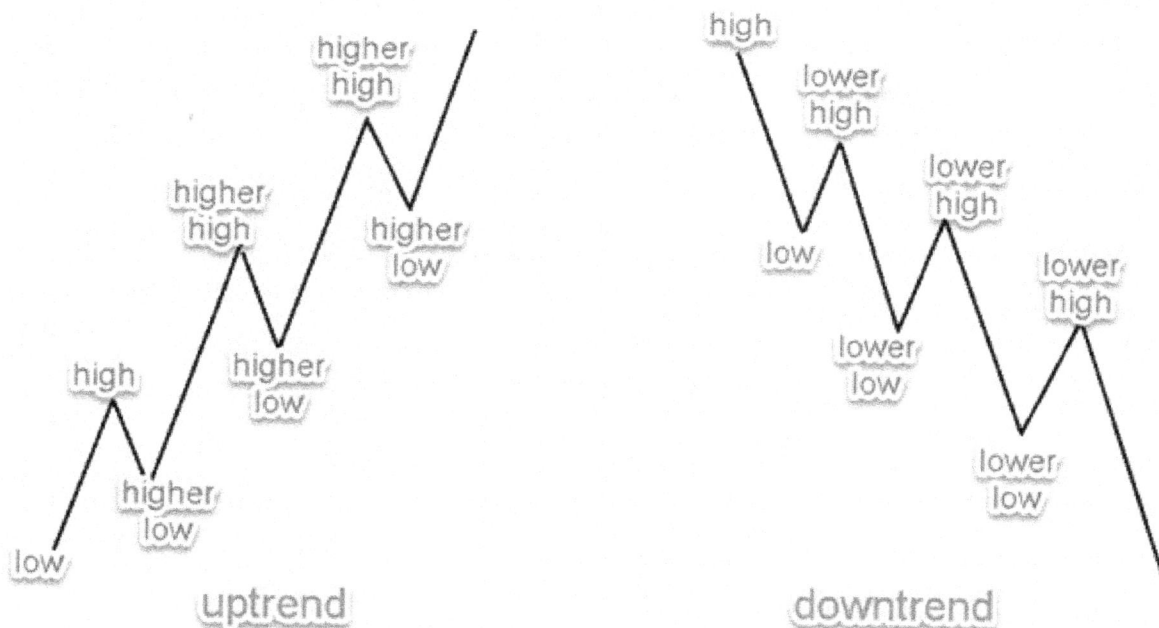

Basically, in an uptrend, the market forms higher highs and higher lows. Thus, when the market fails to create a higher high, there might be some problems with the uptrend momentum. You should look for some other confirmation signals to identify a sell setup and trigger. We will discover this technique in detail later in this book.

On the contrary, if the market is in a downtrend, it creates lower highs and lower lows. Hence, if for some reason the market fails to form a lower low, there might be some problems with the bears' strength. We should watch for a buy signal at those times.

Although we are talking about two opposite trends in the market, the technique is similar. In other words, if you can apply what I share about trading in an uptrend (i.e., trading a reversal from a downtrend to an uptrend), you will be confident in trading in a downtrend using the same principle.

For a simple trend determination, bear in mind:

- *A minimum condition for an uptrend to form is ONE higher high and TWO higher lows. In general, the more highs and lows that follow this pattern, the stronger the trend is.*

- *Similarly, a minimum condition for a downtrend to form is TWO lower highs and ONE lower low. The more highs and lows that follow this pattern, the stronger the trend is.*

These definitions are based on my reversal trading techniques that have been developed through the years. Later in this book, you will fully grasp why I set these criteria for a reliable trend determination method.

Also notice that in a downtrend, the upcoming lower high might retest the newest low on the chart. On the other hand, in an uptrend, the upcoming higher low might revisit the latest high on the chart. The principle here is simple: In trading, support can turn into resistance, and vice versa.

Take a look at the example below.

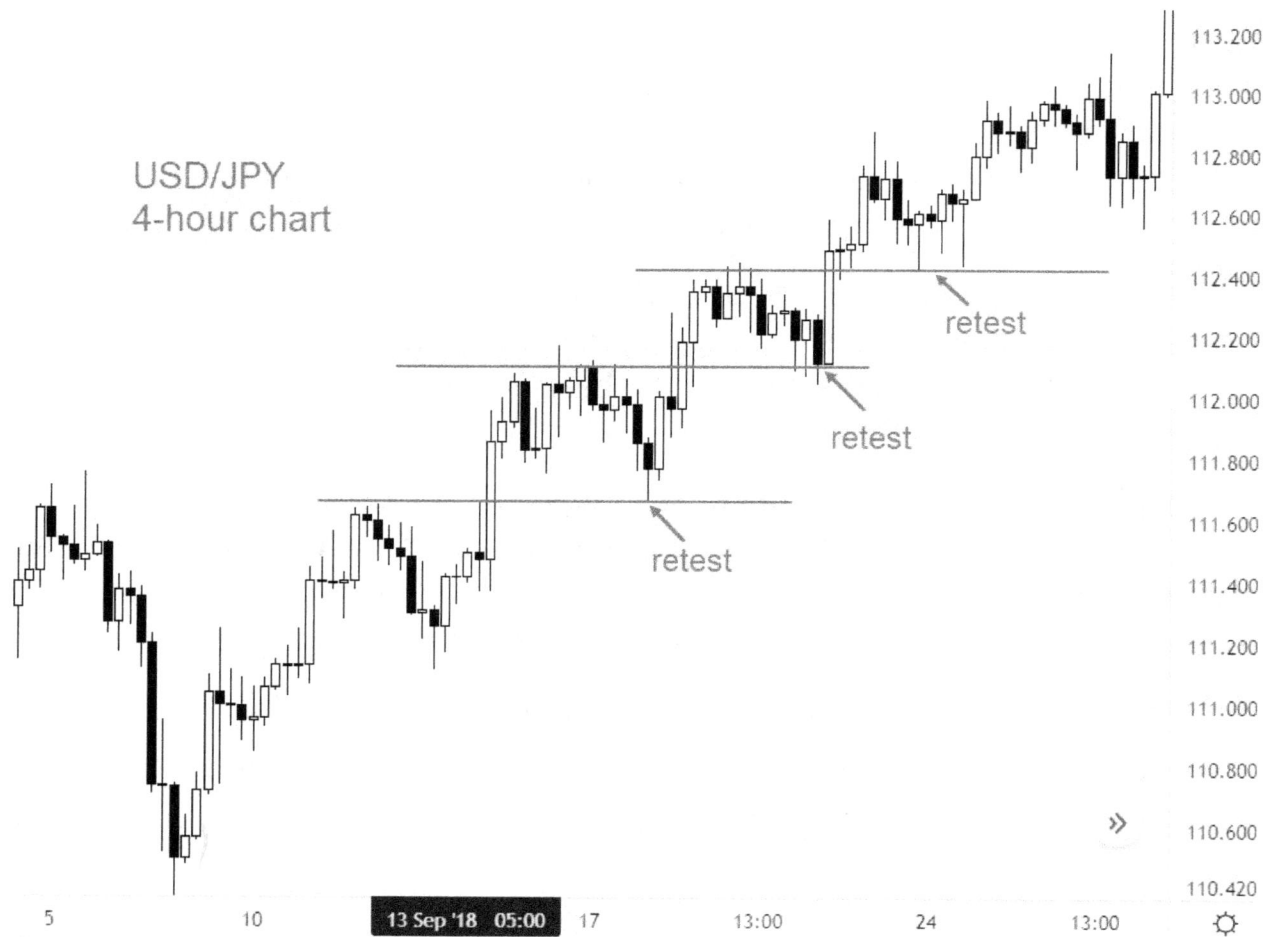

USD/JPY
4-hour chart

retest

retest

retest

In this uptrend, you can see how the market tends to retest the latest support area which is drawn from the latest peak (until the time of the retest) before bouncing back upward. Such retest plays a very important role in determining the entry point, bringing us an ideal risk/reward ratio. In the following chapters, we will dig deeper into retests and the underlying reasons for using them.

2. Non-trend market

A non-trend market, also known as a sideways market, appears when the prices constantly move between a support area and a resistance area. Notice I use the word "area" instead of a specific price level. Using a price area gives us a wider range of price movement on the chart and saves us from missing good opportunities amid wild fluctuations of the price. Let's look at the chart below:

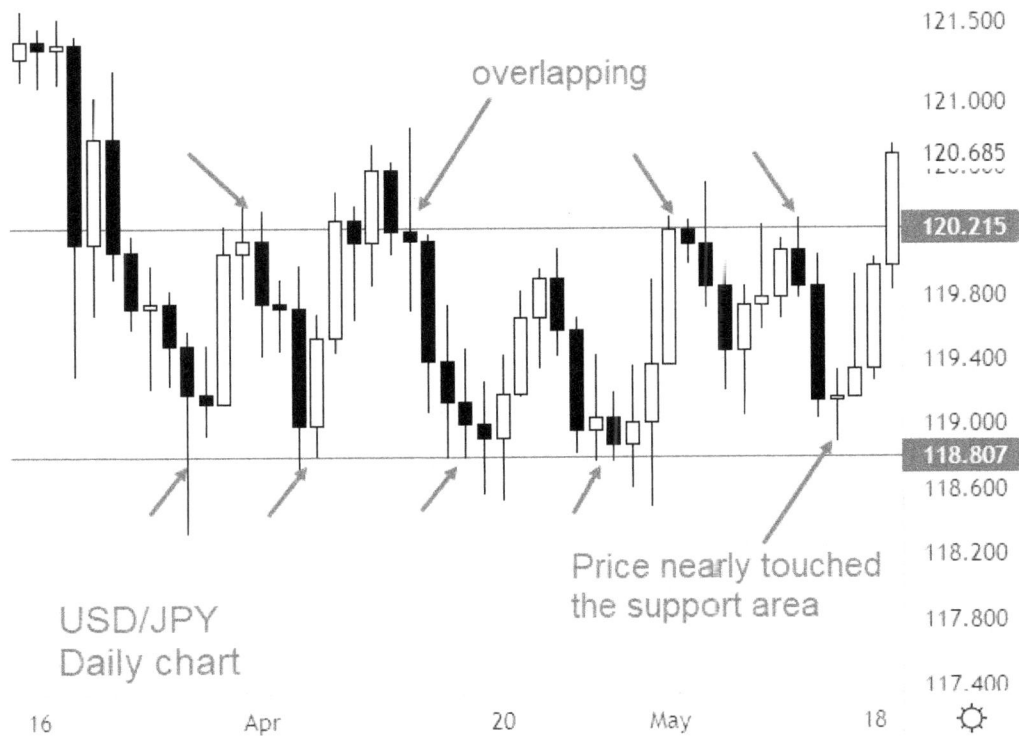

USD/JPY
Daily chart

This is the USD/JPY daily chart. You can easily see that the prices were constantly moving in a range formed by two super-strong bands. By determining key zones instead of fixed price levels, traders could maximize their profits trading sideways. There are some overlapping candlesticks on the chart while one is just about to touch the key support level. These cases are completely normal in any financial trading chart. For example, while we can see how strong the 118.80 was as a support area, there was one point where the price missed just a few pips for a validated visit to the price level. If you treat this level as an area and allow certain tolerance, chances are that you wouldn't miss that buy opportunity.

In the financial markets, I am not a big fan of sideways trading. Yet, if you are interested in this type of market, I recommend the use of key areas in connection with some other important tools.

Note: *In this book, you may see I use the phrases "support/resistance line" or "support/resistance level" from time to time. Please don't misunderstand that I am mentioning a specific price level. I always recommend using "areas" for determining support/resistance.*

As I stated above, determining market trends depends on which timeframes we use. To me, the weekly and daily charts are the best ones for providing a better picture of the market. You should avoid using short timeframes for the identification, such as a 5-minute chart or 30-minute chart.

Also, it is important to note that no trend can last forever. It is always advisable to jump into a trend during its beginning so that we can have the chance to ride most of the trend. To do this, traders must first seek some reliable signals of a trend termination before looking for some signs of a new trend and going with the new trend. This is also known as detecting overbought or oversold areas in the chart, which is by no means an easy task. In the following chapters, I am going to disclose my favorite methods of trading reversals securely and effectively.

CHAPTER VI: SECRETS ON IDENTIFYING RELIABLE MARKET REVERSALS

As a trading mentor, I have seen many traders applying candlestick patterns in a rigid way, leading to many unexpected losses. Those losses are likely to cause emotional pain and severe disasters for traders.

For example, suppose you buy an asset just because a bullish engulfing pattern appears. Or if you are more careful, you place a long order when this pattern is present at a support area.

That's not enough. Trading is not as simple as that. There are many ways you can gain a better understanding of what the market wants to say, ideally through analyzing candlestick patterns and the connections between them.

You may have read some books guiding you through how to trade with candlestick patterns such as pin bars, engulfing patterns, double tops, etc. You were taught how and when to enter trades, how to set stop loss and profit-taking targets. Yet, the financial markets are notorious for their unpredictability, and you can easily encounter a loss if you fail to put these patterns into the right trading context. Your task as a trader is to filter only high probability trade setups, which is what seasoned traders pay much attention to. They carefully judge each trade opportunity in the market, understanding that such prudence will benefit them in the long term.

Reversal trading is closely connected with some popular candlestick patterns like the ones mentioned above. Yet, before diving deeply into these patterns, let's identify some conditions for a reversal to be validated:

- First, the price needs to be presented in a key support or resistance area. (COMPULSORY).
- Second, there is a change of the **market structure**, i.e., from an uptrend to a downtrend, or from a downtrend to an uptrend. (COMPULSORY).
- Third, the candlestick pattern itself must carry a clear sign of a turnaround in connection with market structure analysis (more on this later).

Now, let's dig deeper into these points.

First, finding key support/resistance is highly recommended, but not a "must". While not all reversals start from a key level, it's safer and easier to analyze a turnaround from a primary price zone on the chart. The underlying idea is simple: A key level is where many traders set their take-profit targets.

For example, let's say the trend is bullish and buyers are adding up their positions until the price hits a resistance level. This level is where buyers tend to close their positions or sell their assets, not to mention that other traders may also jump on board with the new trend and take the price much lower. This explains why key levels are ideal places for the price to make a reversal.

Remember just because the price reaches a key level doesn't mean it will change its direction right away. There are probably a few fluctuations around the level, represented by some corrections of the price. In these cases, it's better to explore the chart in a shorter timeframe, which brings you a better idea of whether a reversal can be expected in the near future. We will go into detail about it very soon.

Second, a change in the market structure is a "must" to better increase the chances of picking up a high probability reversal setup.

As we learned in the previous chapter, a sustainable trend is represented by consecutive higher highs and higher lows (in an uptrend) or consecutive lower highs and lower lows (in a downtrend). Thus, a failure to remain in the structure may signal a change in the trend. Look at the picture below for a better illustration:

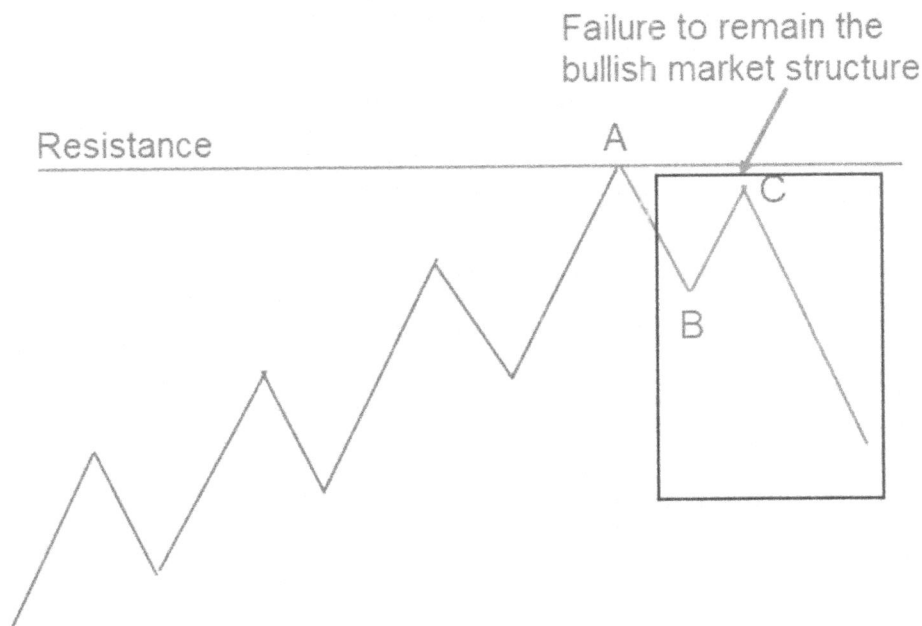

Failure to remain the bullish market structure

Resistance A

C

B

In this chart, an uptrend is in place, with consecutive higher highs and lows, until it reaches a resistance level. A top is formed at A, followed by a low at B. Until B, everything is on track and bull traders can still expect another high that breaks above the resistance level to confirm a possible continuation of the trend.

However, things are not that ideal. The market forms a lower high at C (compared to A). From this point, a downtrend emerges and the initial "higher high & higher low" structure has officially been terminated.

Things work similarly in a downtrend, where the break of the initial "lower highs, lower lows" structure is the first sign of a reversal to the upside of the market.

This is what I mean by "**a change in the market structure**".

Now that we've identified what the break of a market structure looks like, let's dig into the most exciting and interesting part of this book: the breakdown of the market structure secrets. Without knowing these secrets, you may have difficulties in realizing the truth behind seemingly easy-to-understand candlestick movements.

MARKET STRUCTURE – UPTREND TO DOWNTREND

Criteria:

- The market fails to create a higher high. This (not any other criterion) should be the first sign of tiredness of buyers pushing the price higher.
- The price breaks the last low in the initial uptrend.
- The market successfully creates two lower highs in the new downtrend, and the second high must not be higher than the last low in the previous uptrend.

Let's take a look at the hypothetical example below for a better illustration:

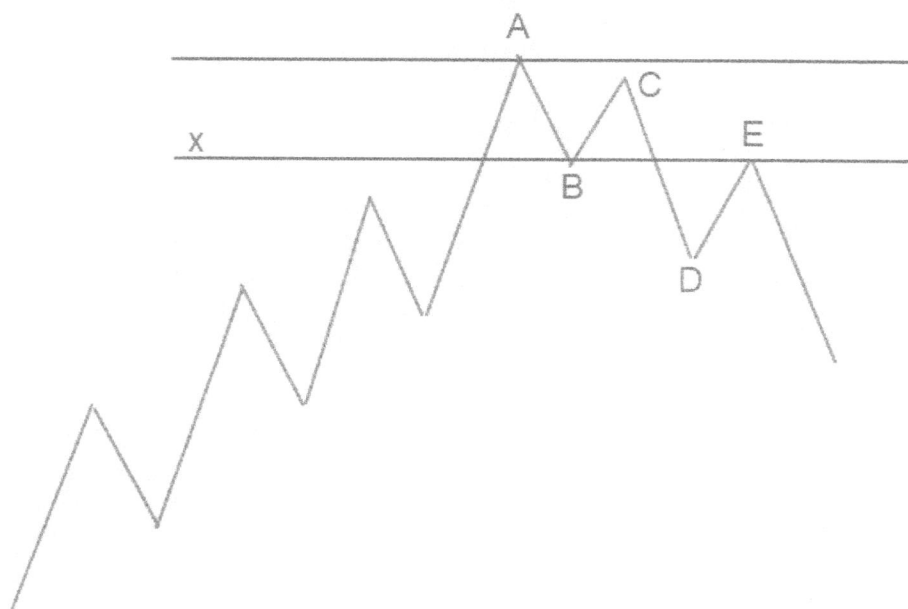

From the example, we can see:

First, the market fails to create a higher high than A. In fact, C could be at the same or lower price than A. It would be better if C is located at a lower level than A. The underlying reason is that selling strength is so strong at the resistance that the chance for buyers to compete is quite low.

Secondly, the price breaks the X line, which is drawn from the last low in the uptrend (B), creating a lower low at D.

Lastly, the market successfully creates two lower highs at C and E, in which E is not higher than B.

Now, let's come to a popular misleading pattern that you should watch out for:

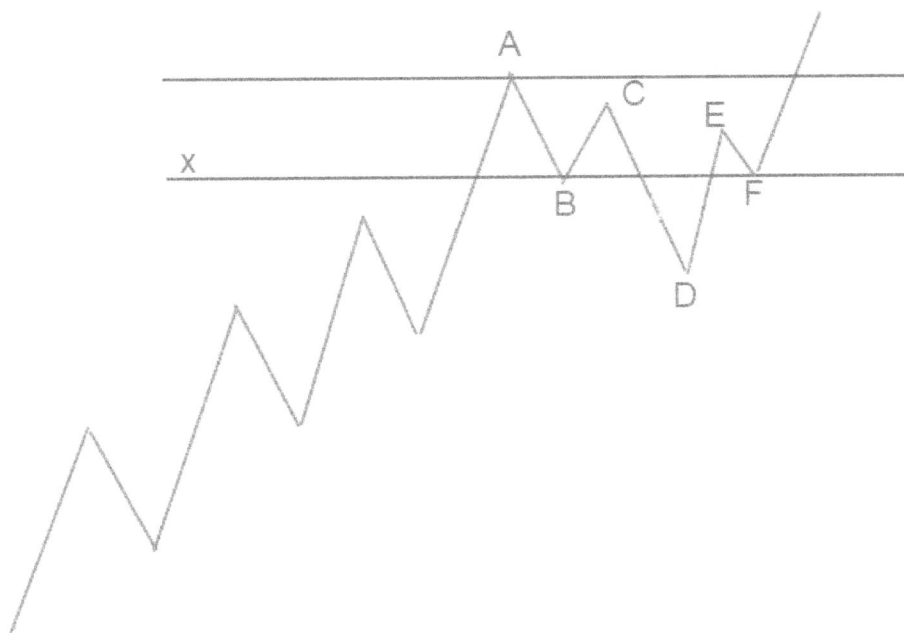

In this example, the third criterion is not satisfied. Although the market forms two lower highs than A (at C and E), the second lower high (E) is higher than the last low during the uptrend (B). This may pave the way for another retest at F before an increase. In these cases, it is advisable to stay on the sideline and watch for other reliable market signals.

MARKET STRUCTURE – DOWNTREND TO UPTREND

Similarly, below are three conditions signaling a possible change from a downtrend to an uptrend:

- The market fails to create a lower low. This (not any other criterion) should be the first sign of tiredness of sellers dragging the price lower.
- The price breaks the last high in the initial downtrend.
- The market successfully creates two higher lows in the new uptrend, and the second low must not be lower than the last high of the previous downtrend.

Although these three signals are opposite to the ones in connection with a change from an uptrend to a downtrend, they are all based on the same principle. Thus, for a quick reference, let's call these three above bullet points the "**3MS principle**" (3 Market Structure). Later on, when I mention the "3MS principle", just understand that I am referring to three conditions for a market structure's change, either from up to down or vice versa.

Once again, it is better you write it down for easy reference later.

Now, let's see what an ideal market structure change from a downtrend to an uptrend looks like:

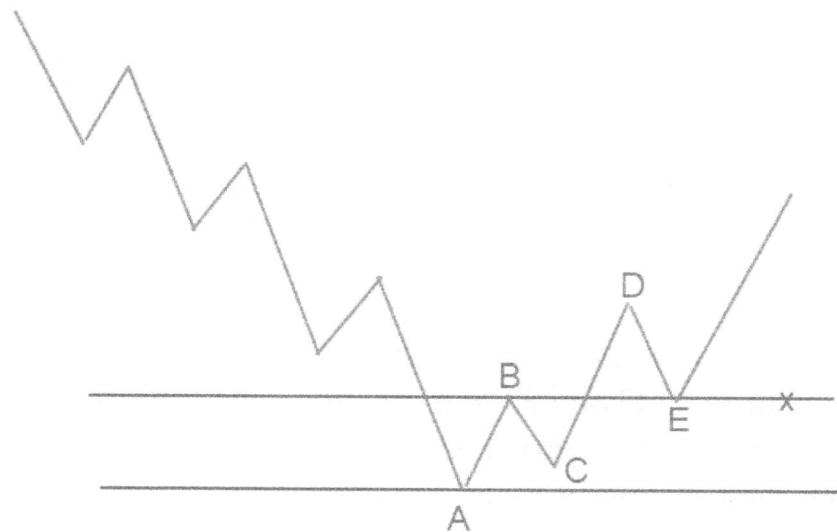

From the picture:

First, the market fails to create a lower low than A. C could be at the same or a higher price than A. It would be ideal if C is located a little bit higher than A as we can see in the picture.

Secondly, the price breaks the last high during the previous downtrend (B), forming a higher high at D.

Lastly, the market successfully creates two higher lows at C and E, in which E is not lower than B.

Similar to the previous examples, you should be careful when the 3MS principles are not fully satisfied, especially the last criterion. Let's take a look at the below picture:

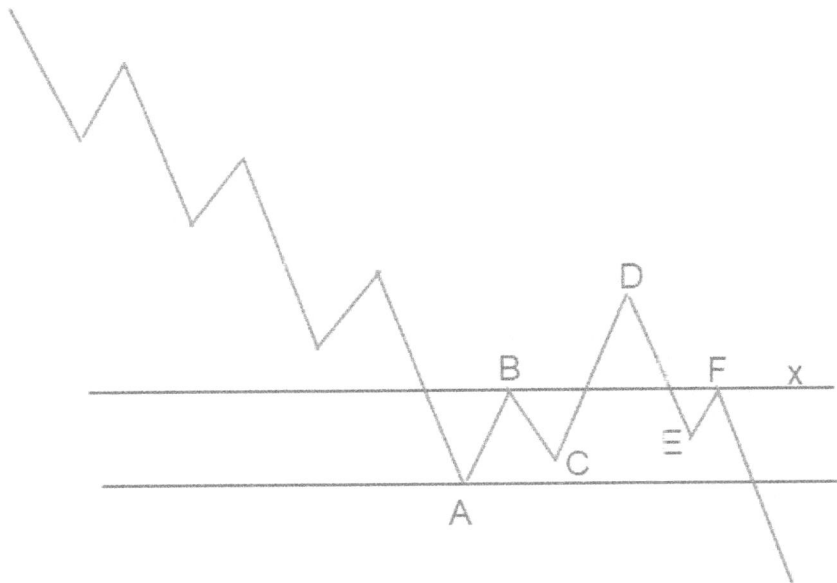

In this example, one problem arises. Although the market forms two higher lows than A (at C and E), the second higher low (E) is lower than the last high in the previous downtrend (B). This may pave the way for another retest at F before a plummet. In those cases, it is better not to enter any trade and wait for more market signals.

In terms of trading reversal, normally I won't open a position until all the 3MS principles appear in the chart. This is not to refute the fact that sometimes, we just need two or even one out of the three components for a successful trade. Sometimes, it depends on your trading style for entering and exiting trades. Being a conservative trader, I prefer the presence of all three. The more signals we gain for our trades, the better we are at stacking the odds in our favor.

Notes: The financial market is unpredictable and nothing is written in stone. There may be some variations in real trading that don't refute the 3MS principle above.

For example, in trading a reversal from an uptrend to a downtrend, the market will not always retest the level at E. It may try to revisit, but sometimes the selling pressure is so strong that it drags the price quicker than expected to the downside. Another variation is the time the market hovers around the resistance level before breaking the latest support level. Things are similar when you're looking for an emerging uptrend. Take a look at the picture below.

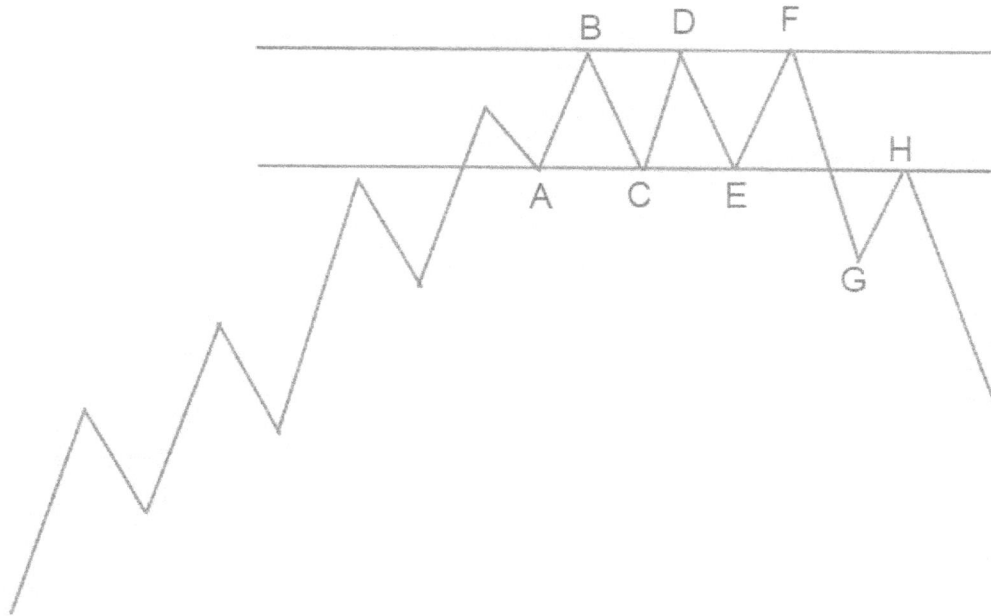

In this hypothetical example, when the price approaches the resistance level, it moves between a small range (from A to F) for a while before breaking the support line and dropping to the zone below it. While the formation resembles the principles we've learned in some ways, traders must be patient to wait for G to be formed.

Some traders may choose to trade sideways in these cases, but it's quite dangerous because there won't be so much room for the price to bounce upward and downward. I'm not a big fan of sideways trading, partly because it's much riskier than trading with a clear and sustainable trend.

So, we have scanned through two out of three criteria in identifying a market reversal. Regarding the third criterion, which relates to the reversal signals within the candle itself, we will take a look at some real examples in the following chapters.

In short, we've learned one of the most important parts of trading market reversals. But it's just part of the process. In the following chapters, we will continue to discover some fatal mistakes traders often make in trading candlestick patterns and how to avoid them. All are presented with real examples.

CHAPTER VII: ENGULFING PATTERN TRADING WITH 3MS PRINCIPLE

An "engulfing pattern" is one of my favorite trading setups. Like many other trading patterns, engulfing patterns are categorized into bullish engulfing bars and bearish engulfing bars.

A bullish engulfing pattern, as its name implies, signals a potential move to the upside. It happens when a long bullish candlestick fully engulfs the previous bearish bar. The open price of the engulfing candlestick could be lower (ideally) or equal to the previous one's close.

By contrast, a bearish engulfing pattern signals a potential move to the downside. It happens when a long bearish candlestick fully engulfs the previous upward bar. The open price of this engulfing candlestick could be higher (ideally) or equal to the previous one's close.

Take a look at the following picture for an illustration:

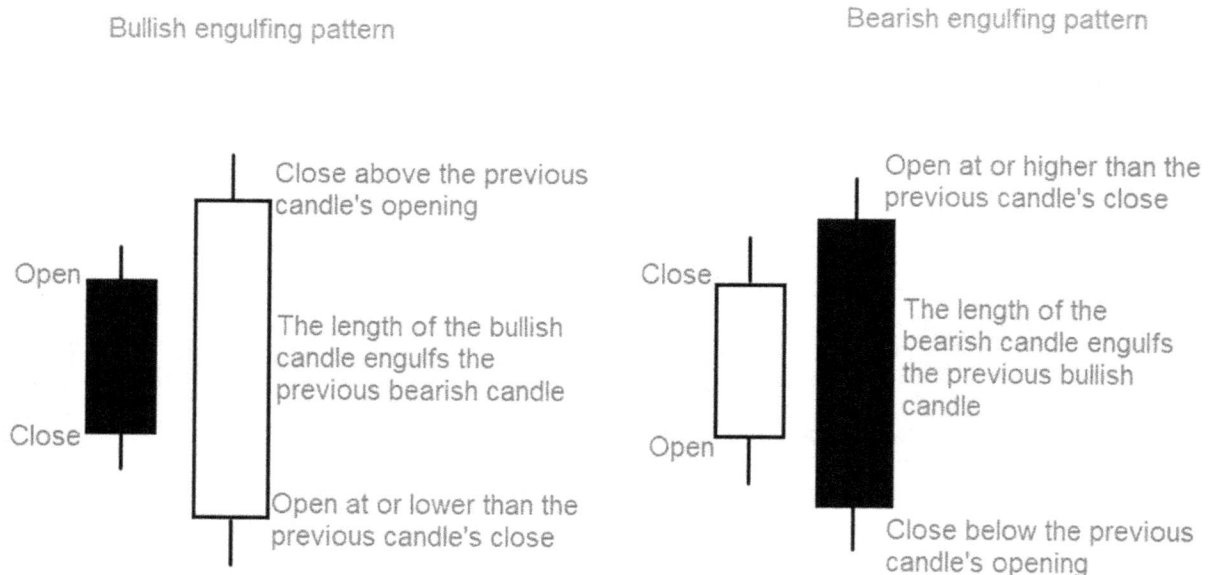

Identifying a reliable engulfing bar may greatly help traders in finding a high probability trade entry. Yet, there are a lot of false engulfing signals in the market that can easily cost traders money if they fail to analyze carefully.

Look at the picture below:

As we can see from the EUR/AUD chart, the market formed a strong resistance level at 1.5080 (the horizontal line) before the engulfing pattern appeared (see the first arrow). Notice when the price first visited the level, it drastically bounced to the downside, which confirmed the 1.5080 level was a key area. You can see the resistance remains unbreakable three more times before turning into a strong support area later (the last arrow).

Notice the engulfing pattern in the chart which is not present at a key support or resistance level, meaning the chance for a reversal is not so high. In other words, it fails to meet the first condition of a potential reversal. In those cases, it's advisable to stay on the sideline until the price approaches a key level. As we've learned, those key levels provide a higher chance of a turnaround.

Let's look at another example when an engulfing pattern that does not meet all entry criteria may bring unexpected losses to traders.

1.52000
1.50800
1.50000
1.48000
1.47182
1.46000
1.44500
1.43000
1.41500
1.40000
1.38800
1.37600

False engulfing pattern
(although it is present at
a key level)

EUR/AUD
Daily chart

03 May '17   15   Jun   19   Jul   17

Still, with the EUR/AUD daily chart and the 1.5080 key level, an engulfing bar was present at a major resistance area, which meets the first condition of a potential turnaround. However, it failed to break the upward market structure. The picture below gives us a better idea of how things look in a shorter timeframe.

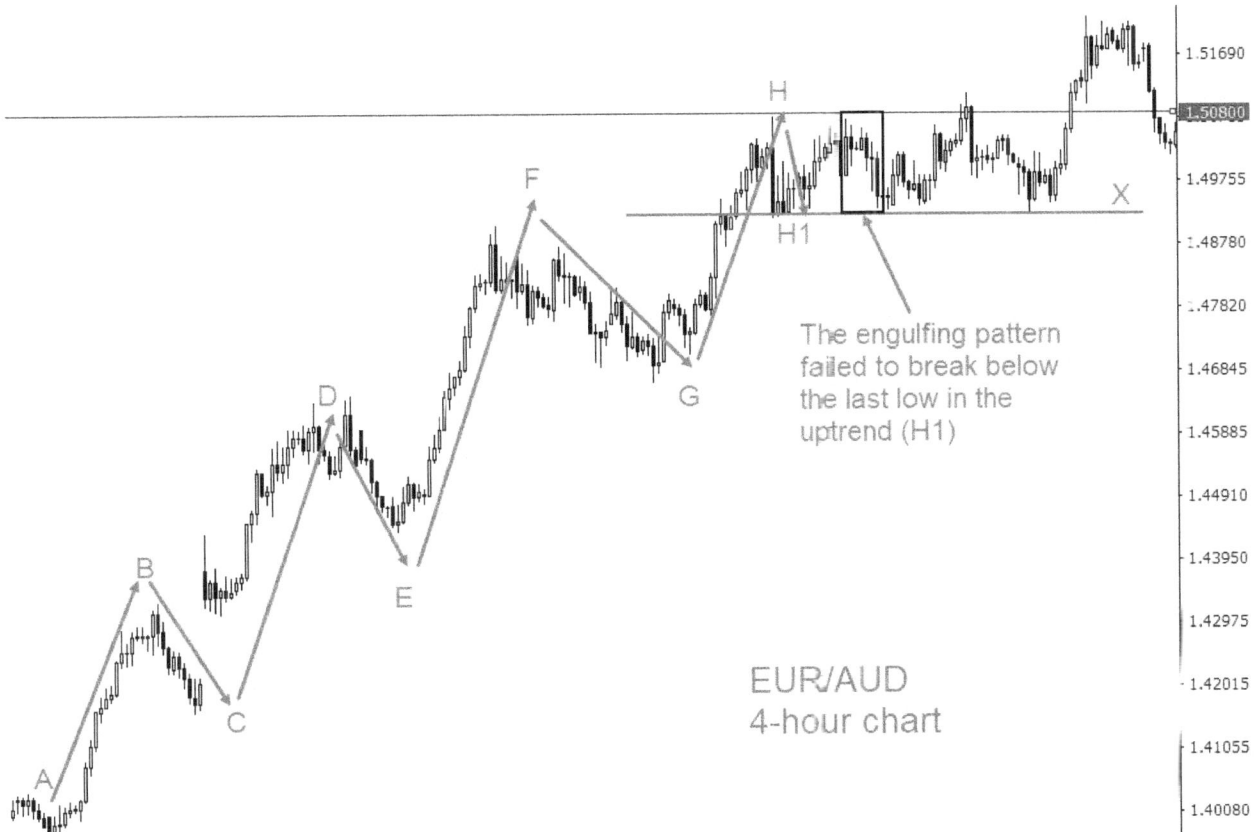

The engulfing pattern
failed to break below
the last low in the
uptrend (H1)

EUR/AUD
4-hour chart

In the 4-hour chart, things are much clearer. First, please note that the daily engulfing pattern is in the small rectangle in the picture.

At first glance, we can see the market was forming a strong bullish trend from A to H. Afterwards, the H1 low was formed during the process. From H1, the market failed to create a higher high than H, signaling that the bulls were taking a rest. However, we have yet to gather any reliable confirmation of a downtrend. Remember a minimum condition for a downtrend to form is the creation of at least two lower highs and one lower low (as mentioned in the previous chapters). In this example, if we treat H as the first high and H1 as the first low in a downtrend, then we are lacking one lower low and two lower highs.

H

F

D

B

C

A

E

G

H1

X

The engulfing pattern
failed to break the
latest low on the chart
(H1)

EUR/AUD
4-hour chart

1.51690

1.50800

1.49755

1.48780

1.47820

1.46845

1.45885

1.44910

1.43950

1.42975

1.42015

1.41055

1.40080

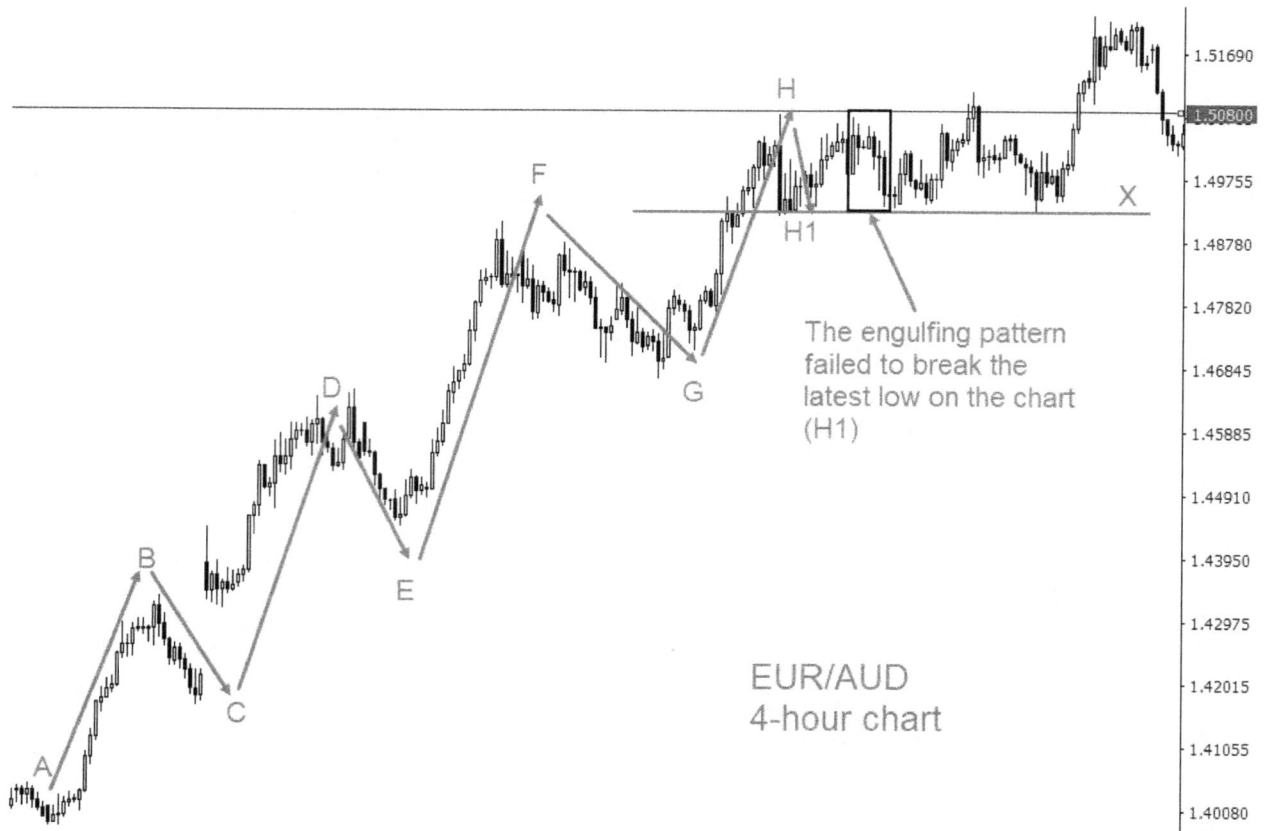

Moreover, let's focus on the X level drawn from the latest low (H1). Notice that it held strong as a support level which denied the bears' pressure several times. This indicates that the market structure still remained unchanged, i.e., the uptrend still prevailed at least until the close of the daily engulfing pattern. Put differently, the selling pressure was not strong enough to win against the bulls' force. When we observe the 4-hour chart, it is obvious that the above-mentioned engulfing candlestick did not carry in it any signs of a reversal in connection with market structure. In other words, the pattern failed to meet the second and the third condition of a validated reversal.

If you don't understand the underlying market structure using a shorter timeframe, you may feel something of a betrayal when a considered profitable pattern doesn't work. However, once you know that it fails to meet two out of three preset criteria for a potential trade setup, you can relax and watch the candlesticks move without wrapping yourself in negative emotions.

Trading any reversal after successfully confirming all three conditions increases the probability of trade success. Below is another example of a bullish engulfing pattern present at a key support level but fails to start a reversal.

On the daily timeframe, things might be ideal for a turnaround to the upside...

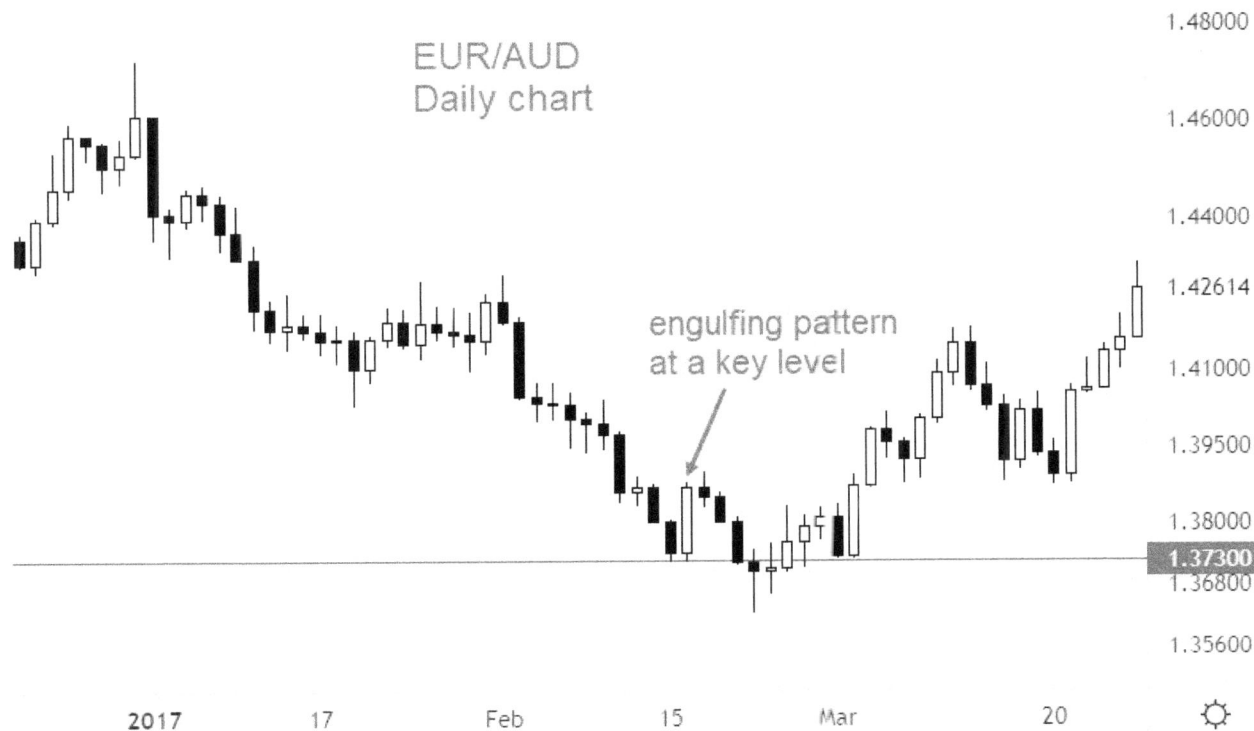

EUR/AUD
Daily chart

engulfing pattern
at a key level

However, if you had entered a buy entry right after the engulfing bar, you would have encountered a loss. Let's see what happened on the 4-hour chart below.

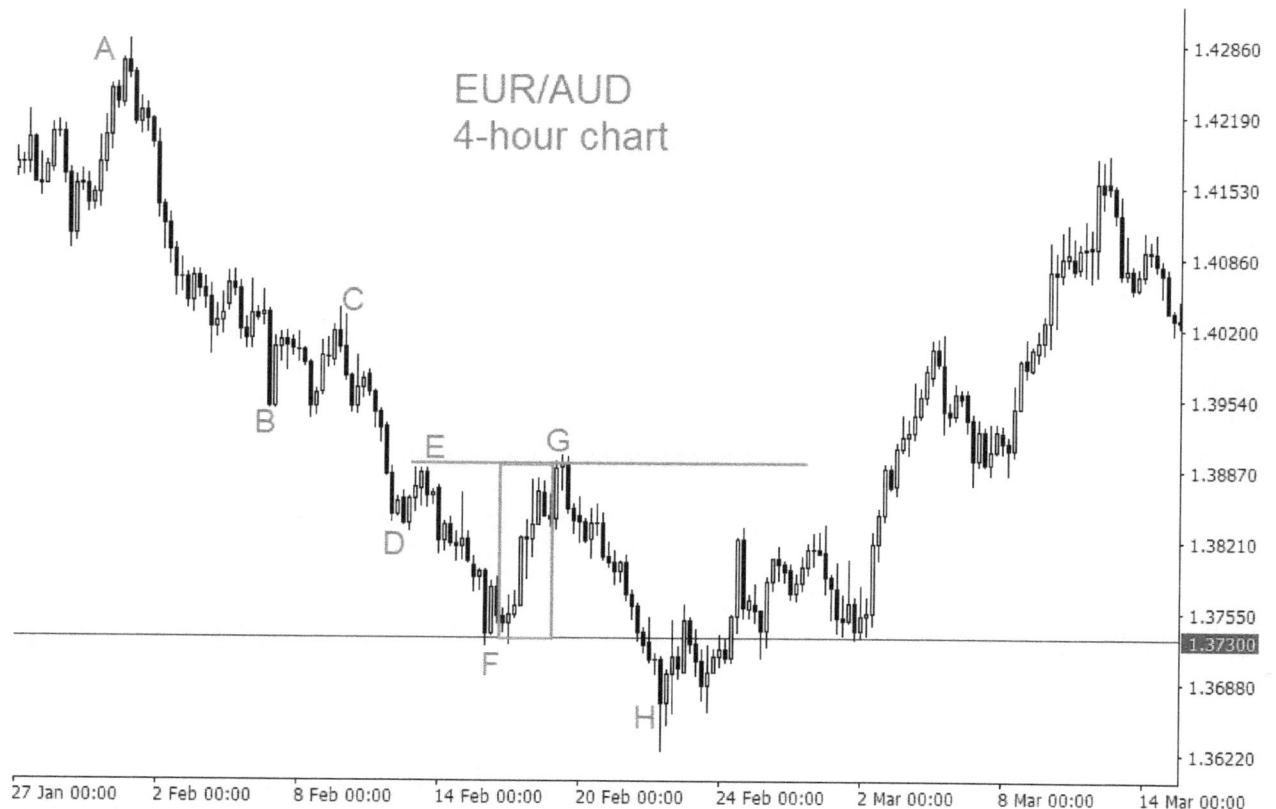

EUR/AUD
4-hour chart

Note that the daily bullish engulfing pattern is comprised of a few 4-hour candlesticks in the rectangle.

Still based on the 3MS method of analyzing the market, we all see the engulfing bar is located in a key support zone, which satisfies the first condition of a reversal.

As we can see, the market was in a clear downtrend from A to F, forming lower highs and lower lows. Then, the bullish engulfing bar tried to break the dominant trend by preventing the market from forming a lower low. Unfortunately, it failed to close above E – the latest lower high at that time. This failure indicated that no change in the market structure was made, thus any ideas of buying the currency pair should be re-considered. You can see how the market continued its strong downtrend and formed a lower low at H. An uptrend had not been formed until several 4-hour candlesticks later. Once again, the second and third criteria of a reversal were not satisfied in this engulfing candlestick. Trading right after the appearance of this bullish bar would put you in great danger.

Let's analyze what happened next to find an ideal trade entry that meets all three conditions of a potential reversal.

Look at the picture below:

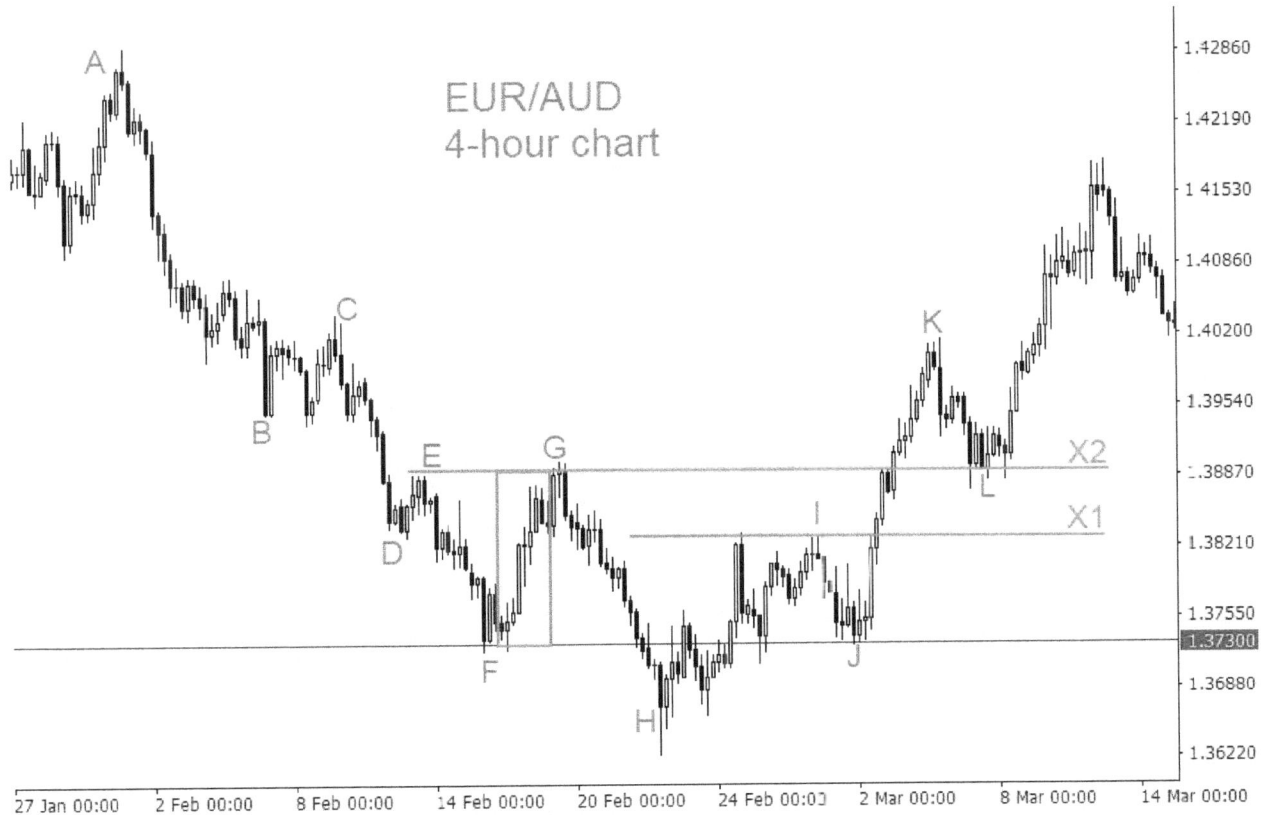

The market continued to make a lower high at I (compared to G). The problem with the downtrend started when the market failed to create a lower low at J. This tells us that, when approaching a strong support zone, the sellers were encountering a strong opposing force from the bulls. They then lost the battle at J, where the price failed to make a lower low. Should you be in a position like this, be prepared for a buy signal.

The market's effort to touch the previous key support zone at J (before shooting up) could also be seen as a retest before a potential uptrend. Trading on retests has always been my favorite style regarding many types of assets or instruments.

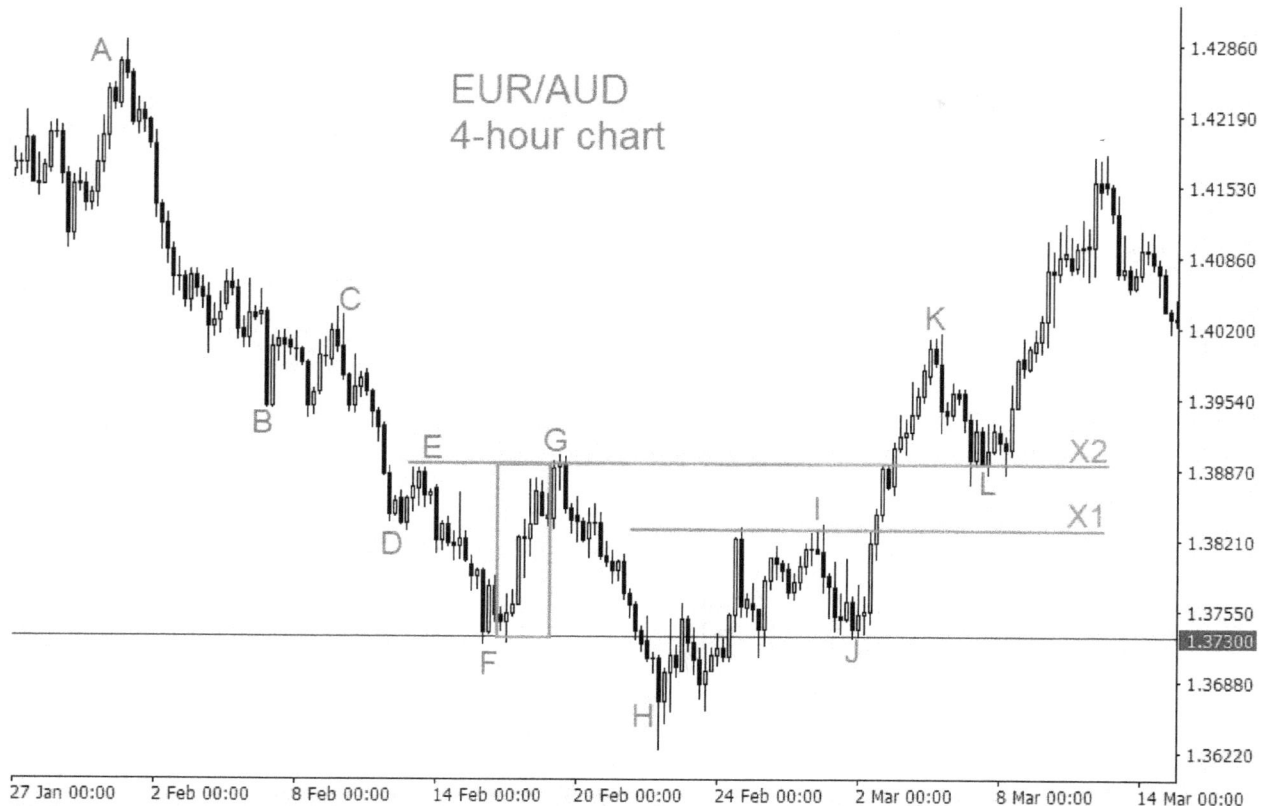

EUR/AUD
4-hour chart

When analyzing any market structure, for example from a downtrend to an uptrend, the break of the last high (in the previous downtrend) plays a very important part in whether we should enter a trade or not. In this case, notice that from J, the price strongly broke the X1 level, meaning that the nearest high (till that time) was broken. The break then results in a higher high at K, the second high during a (new) uptrend.

There we have it. Notice that after the market created another low at L, it was then having two higher lows (J and L) and one higher high (K), which meets the second 3MS principle. A change in the market structure was confirmed by L, and L is not lower than I (the third 3MS principle). Note that in this case, the price didn't visit the X1 line, but did touch the X2 line – a closer support level. This is completely acceptable. Trading should not be too rigid.

Some traders may be concerned about whether or not we should wait for the price to form a higher low at L for an entry, or why we shouldn't enter a trade right after it breaks the nearest resistance from J.

Below are the two reasons L could be an ideal price level to initiate an order.

- This is the art of trading on a retest. Except for a highly volatile market like cryptocurrency where sometimes the price may skyrocket quickly without looking back, a retest gives you a better position to enter a trade. Let's use a simple rubber ball as an example. Imagine how the ball quickly bounces back after strongly hitting the floor. This is how the price works. It often needs a strong base for a substantial climb or drop. Before a rally or plummet, it's better to look for a correction of the overall trend. Technically speaking, it is when buyers or sellers are recharging their energy for an imminent powerful move.

- When a support level is broken, it is likely to turn into a resistance level, and vice versa. Let's see how the X2 line became a strong resistance area when it hindered the price from breaking above it, forming E and G. After being broken, it turned into support and prices tended to revisit the X2 level. Hence, it's better to initiate a trade on a retest. The worst outcome of waiting for a retest? Missing a trade.

There is no need to worry if you know there are unlimited opportunities ahead.

And most importantly, your capital is still safely protected.

Coming back to the daily timeframe, the break of the X1 line was clearly illustrated by the second engulfing bar. A strong upward trend was followed by that candlestick. Now, the third criterion for a potential reversal pattern was also met.

EUR/AUD
Daily chart

false engulfing pattern

workable engulfing pattern

1.47000
1.46000
1.45000
1.44000
1.43000
1.42000
1.41000
1.40000
1.39200
1.38400
1.37600
1.37300
1.36900
1.36250

14   Mar   20   Apr   17   May

In trading, the more factors you collect in validating your setups, the more probability of success you will have. One of the most powerful tools to confirm a break of the market structure is a trend line.

Look at the USD/CAD chart below.

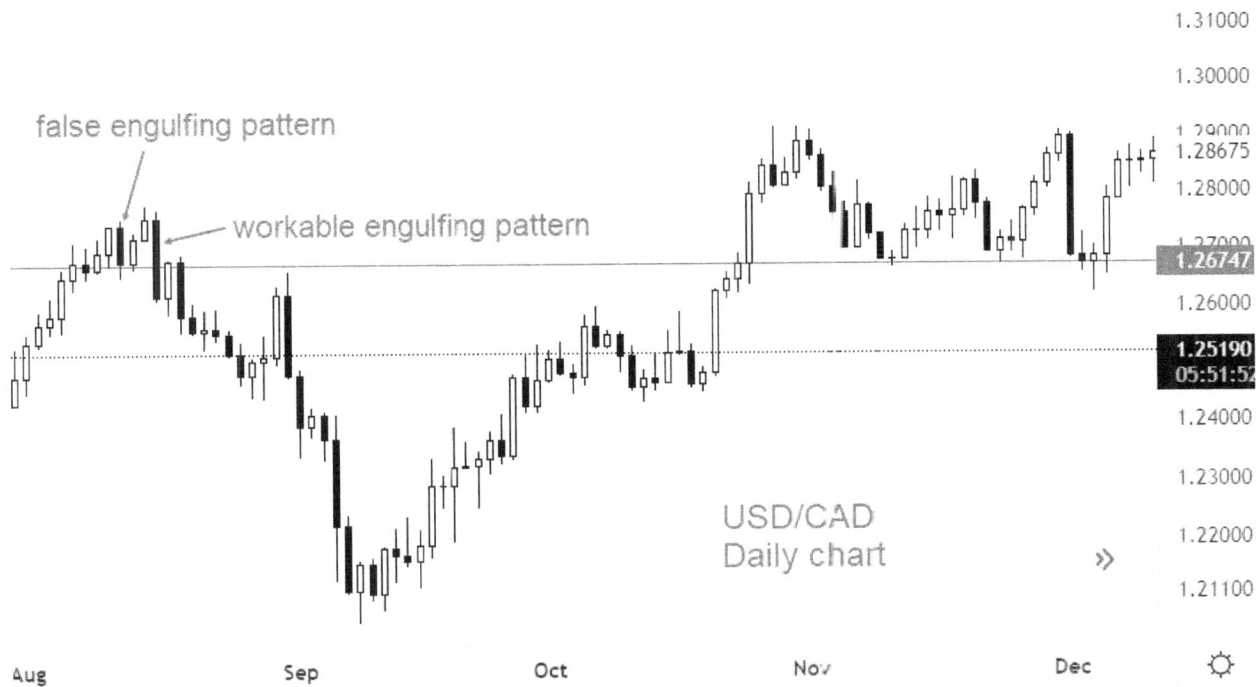

false engulfing pattern

workable engulfing pattern

USD/CAD
Daily chart

In this example, we have two daily bearish engulfing patterns not far away from each other. However, just one of them works as a reversal signal.

Now, let's switch to the 4-hour chart and draw a trend line to see what happens.

USD/CAD
Daily chart

Here it is. Note that the two rectangles indicate two daily engulfing bars on the 4-hour timeframe. First, by using market structure analysis, you can easily explain the first one's failure to drag prices to the below price area, as well as how the second one provided an obvious indication of the seller's potential dominance.

While the two engulfing patterns are located at a key resistance area, their voices on telling market structure's change are different. Applying 3MS principle, it is clear that the first engulfing bar failed to meet all three criteria of a reliable change, which accounts for its failure to start a reversal that time.

USD/CAD
Daily chart

When analyzing the market structure's change in the second engulfing bar, we can see it **strongly broke the last low** during the uptrend (A) and then **formed two lower highs** (C and D) in which the second low (D) was located at a lower level than the latest low before that (B). The highest high during the uptrend is also the highest high during the following downtrend. The 3MS principle is satisfied. The only drawback is that the break of the latest low (at B) came before the failure to form a lower high (at C). Sound a little confusing? Don't worry, we will talk more about this problem in Chapter IX. Anyway, compared to the first engulfing bar, the second one outshines in every aspect, making it a much higher probability trade setup.

Moreover, you can see how the second bearish engulfing bar (the second rectangle) breaks the X1 line on the 4-hour timeframe, indicating that it carries strong downward momentum, not to mention that its body (on the daily chart) is longer than most of the previous candlesticks. All of these characteristics (particularly the former) indicate the pattern itself carries a strong signal of a turnaround in the market. Hence, the third condition of a reversal is met too.

All of these signals show support for the second engulfing bar being the start of a trend reversal.

Moreover, by drawing an upward trend line, it is even clearer the second engulfing candlestick indicates more selling pressure than the first one by strongly breaking the trend line and poking through the X1 zone.

Still, on the example, we can see how trading on a retest can save you in some cases. Notice how the big bearish marubozu (a type of Japanese candlestick with a long body and short shadows) strongly broke the support zone but failed to drag the price to the downside right away. While risk-tolerant traders may choose to enter a trade around the X1 level, I prefer a trade initiation at D. What you should do in each case is not clear in black and white. Yet, I'm in favor of a conservative style and that's why I often (not always) consider entering a trade at D.

In short, it all boils down to this: How traders read signals from the market defines their probability of success in trading. In many cases, traders may not truly understand the underlying reasons behind their losing trades. Applying multi-timeframe analysis could give us a much better idea of when and how we should take action or stay on the sideline. I hope this chapter has brought you some aha moments regarding how to trade with engulfing pattern – the most popular trading pattern on the chart.

CHAPTER VIII: PIN BAR TRADING WITH 3MS PRINCIPLE

Along with engulfing candlesticks, the pin bar is also a commonly occurring pattern on the financial chart. Another name for it is a hammer candlestick, because it resembles a hammer.

The main message in a pin bar is a heated battle is going on between the bulls and the bears, causing a substantial difference between the highest price and the lowest price within a candlestick formation.

Similar to other patterns, pin bars could be divided into bullish ones and bearish ones. A bullish pin bar is represented by a long lower shadow (aka tail) while a bearish hammer is characterized by a long, higher shadow. One important condition to validate a pin bar is that the shadow should be at least twice the real body. Other than that, it's not so important whether the closing price is higher than the opening price or not.

Take a look at the illustration below:

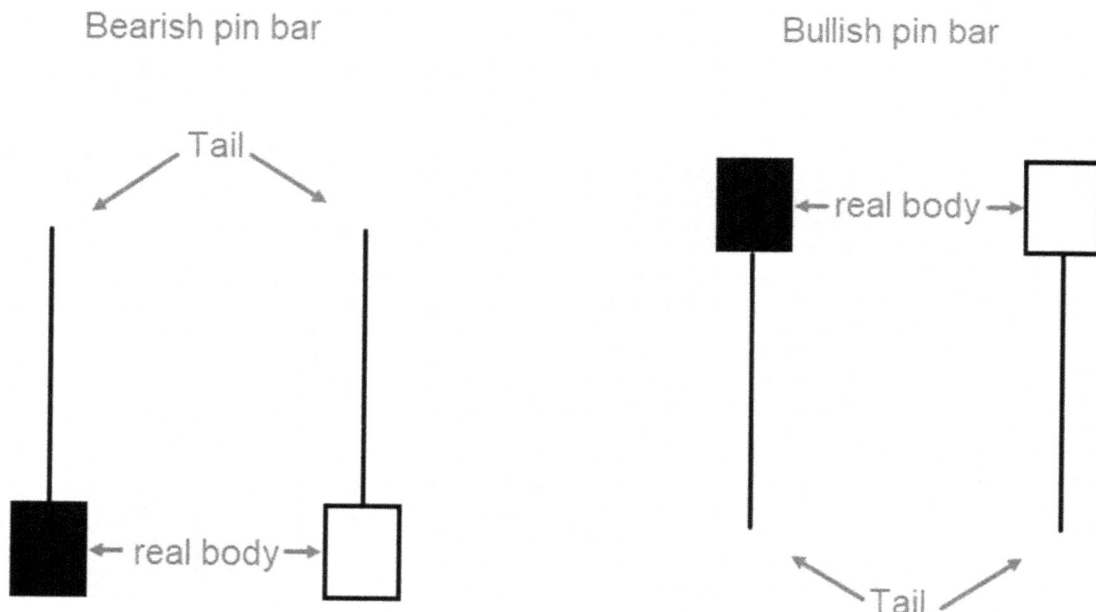

Bearish pin bar

Bullish pin bar

Tail

real body

real body

Tail

Like the engulfing pattern, a high probability pin bar setup is not as easy as many traders often think. As a trader, you need to put any pin bar in a bigger picture, i.e., identify whether the candle indicates a reliable market reversal using the two compulsory conditions of a turnaround discussed previously. Furthermore, you also need to determine (based on the closing price of the pin bar) whether it carries any signal of a reversal in connection with market structure analysis or not. If not, stay on the sideline and wait.

Let's take a look at a daily chart of the GBP/CAD currency pair below:

Notice how a pin bar pattern was present at a key support and resistance area. This level had been tested a few times before without being broken to the upside. This shows how strong the support area was at that time. On the right side of the chart, a pin bar appeared with its close price above the key level. Hence, the first condition is met.

At first glance, trading this pin bar seemed to be a good idea. However, things were not that wonderful. Let's now see what happened next on a shorter timeframe and you may understand more about the success probability of a trade. Below is the four-hour chart of the same pair.

GBP/CAD
4-hour chart

Fail to break the resistance level
drawn from the nearest low

This chart depicts the downtrend before the pin bar was formed.

Note that the mentioned daily pin bar is comprised of six four-hour candlesticks in the rectangle. Also, the last low during the downtrend is defined at X, and we draw a horizontal line from X (the X line) to determine whether the market structure was broken by the pressure from the bulls or not.

As we can see, the pin bar has fueled an upward momentum, shifting the downtrend to a sideways range where the price tended to bounce between the two bands. However, the X line remained unbreakable during the whole short period, meaning the bull's force was not strong enough at that time to initiate a reversal. In this case, just by watching how the price reacted when it approached the X level, we can have a better idea of whether or not there is a high probability of a reversal.

Below is what happened next on the four-hour chart.

bullish momentum
becomes weaker
and weaker

GBP/CAD
4-hour chart

27   Jun   10   17

Contrary to what many traders might expect after the formation of the pin bar, the downward movement could only be slowed for a while instead of being terminated. The buyers couldn't take the price to the X line even once, and then the buying momentum started to die down through time, approving the continuation of the downtrend.

The market structure remained intact. The pin bar became an invalid signal, and traders should look for other opportunities.

Now, let's see what an effective pin bar looks like in the following example:

GBP/JPY
Weekly chart

Ideal pin bar

151.368
150.000
146.000
142.000
140.250
139.000
136.000
133.000
130.500
128.000
125.500
123.300

2017   Mar   Jun   Aug   9

We start with the weekly chart.

Let's pay attention to the pin bar on the chart. Now, when looking at a smaller candlestick than most of the surrounding ones, a lot of traders may doubt its reliability. Just be calm and continue reading.

As I always emphasize, an ideal pin bar (or any other candlestick pattern) should be present in a key support or resistance area before any further consideration. The pin bar we mention here satisfies this criterion. Notice how a lot of previous weekly candlesticks tried to close on the other side of the 140.25 level on the chart, but failed, making it an ideal area to consider a trade setup.

Now, let's move to the daily chart to see what happens:

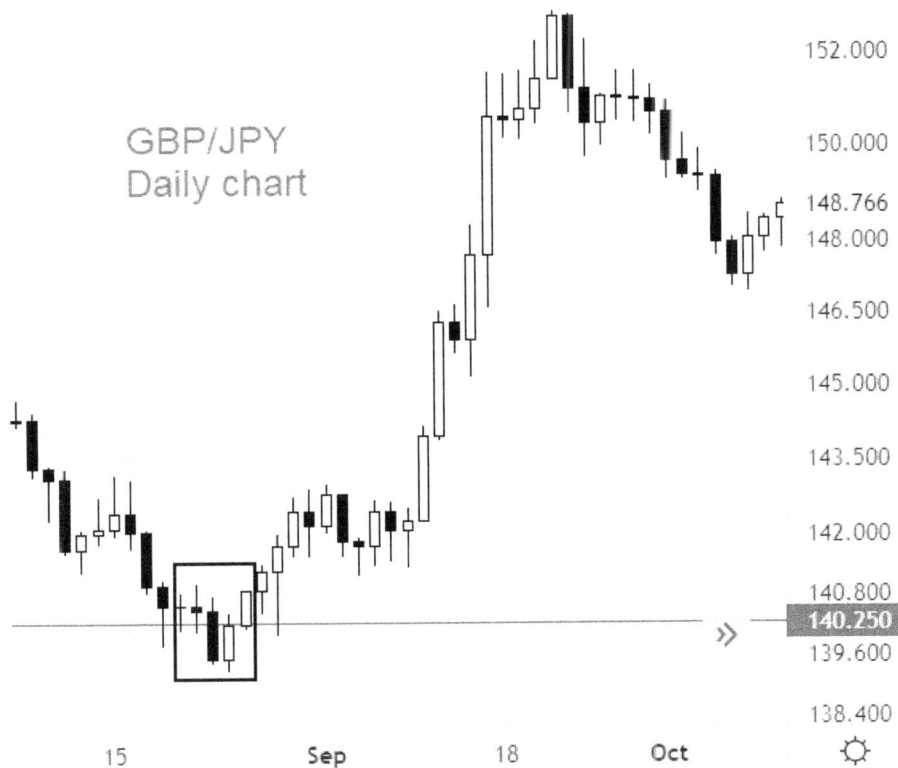

On the daily chart, the weekly bar is comprised of five daily candlesticks in the rectangle. On Wednesday of the week, the market formed a strong bearish candlestick. However, during the two following days, buyers completely dominated the market, making two strong bullish candles that engulfed the prior candlestick. This indicated that at one point, the sellers tried to drag the price lower and maintained the overall trend. However, they seemed to lose their energy and lost the game to buyers, who successfully drove the market to close above the key support area. To gain a deeper understanding of the market structure, let's take a look at the 4-hour chart to see how the buyers managed to control the game.

GBP/JPY
4-hour chart

Let's start the overall downtrend picture with the starting point at A and the ending point at J. The weekly candle was comprised of all 4-hour candles in the rectangle. It was apparent that by the end of the week, the market structure remained unchanged. However, in the following weeks, the market successfully broke the X line drawn from I (the last high during the downtrend). That break **initiated** a change in the market structure from the downtrend to the uptrend, resulting in the formation of K.

GBP/JPY
4-hour chart

Notice how the 3MS principle worked well in this case. While the price **broke the last high** (I) during the previous downtrend and formed the first high in the new uptrend (K), it **failed to create any lower low than J**. As I have stated, a reliable signal of a market structure's change (in this case from a downtrend to an uptrend) must include at least two higher lows (in comparison with the lowest low). As you may observe, after **forming two higher lows at L and N (N was not lower than I** – the last high during the previous downtrend), the market saw a strong rally.

Some people might be in favor of placing a buy order at L when the market failed to break a very strong support area (the long horizontal line). While I admit that signal was quite reliable in some ways (analyzed on a key support zone), I have to make a warning because by trading this way, they are ignoring the last criterion in the 3MS principle (at least 2 higher lows).

Remember, trading is not black and white. In some cases, you may not need all the three components in the 3MS principle for a successful trade. It boils down to how you weigh risks and rewards in your trade option. While trading should be prudent, it should not be too rigid. A buy order at L would be preferred by many traders, and they have reasons to risk there. Sometimes you may have a gut feeling on entering trades and could end up making (big) profits. What I've provided here is a "proven framework" that I believe if you apply consistently, you would stand a good chance of being consistently profitable. Hope you've gotten the point.

Also, I always recommend traders combine more indicators in their market analysis method. Once again, adding a trend line could better stack the odds in our favor. Let's see how the same weekly pin bar successfully broke a strong trend line (a trend line that had been touched many times without being broken) on the 4-hour chart. Take a look at the picture below.

GBP/JPY
4-hour chart

trend line is broken

A very interesting point of the market structure analysis method is that you can trade with pure price action without relying too much on candlestick patterns. In this way, trend line, support/resistance, and retests all play an important role in any trade entry and stop levels.

With that said, I don't mean to ignore technical indicators that are available on many trading software and platforms. What I want to convey is we should combine many market factors (but not too many) to obtain the "confluence" effects from the market. A confluence occurs when at least two indicators/tools turn the light to green for a trade setup or trigger. The more approval we receive from these factors, the better chance we stand to win the trade.

CHAPTER IX: INSIGHTS INTO DOUBLE TOP/BOTTOM TRADING

Along with pin bars and engulfing patterns, double top/bottom patterns are among the high probability trade setups on the chart. In the next sections, we will learn how to identify these patterns on the chart, the underlying reasons behind it, and how to identify the three important orders in each trade: entry price, stop-loss, and take-profit.

1. Reliable conditions for a double top/bottom to work:

- It is positioned at a support/resistance level

As we've discussed, any candlestick pattern must be analyzed in connection with a support/resistance level. In other words, trading candlestick patterns without referring to support/resistance levels could put you in great danger. The stronger any support/ resistance level is (when it is tested many times without being broken), the more reliable it is.

To avoid repetition, let's take a look at the double top pattern. The double bottom pattern is very similar. If you grasp the intention regarding double top trading, applying it to top or bottom patterns would not cause you any problem.

Look at the illustration below:

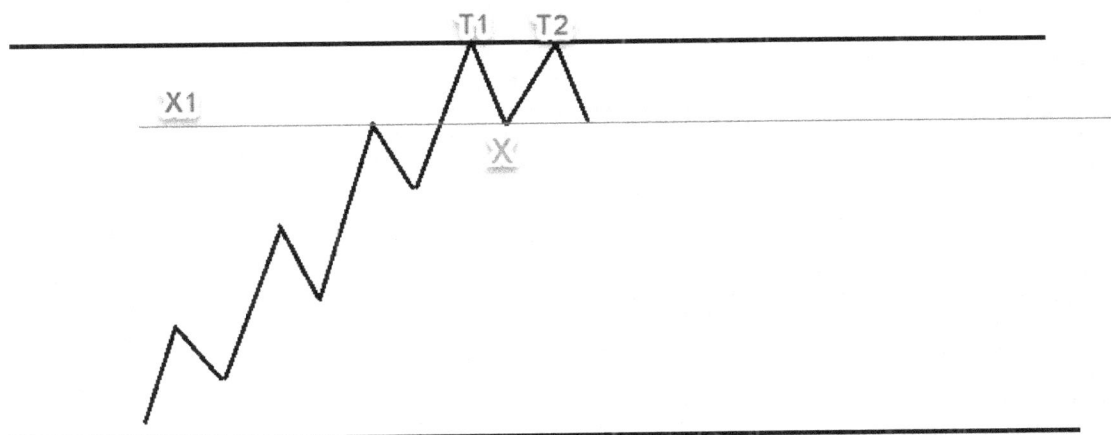

From the picture, the market is in an uptrend before it encounters a key resistance area. From there it creates the first top at T1 before bouncing back to X and forming the second top at T2. In any double top pattern analysis, X is a very important point in determining the entry-level in the market. More on that later. In this case, X1 is called the neckline.

After we have found a double top/bottom pattern situated on a key level, we can look at the market structure next. The market is strong in its uptrend until T2 appears. Before the presence of this "second top", T1 and X play as the newest high and low, and those who are in favor of an uptrend would expect a formation of a higher high than T1. Yet, the second top at T2 negates this scenario and paves the way for a double top to form. Please note that T2 is not necessarily the same height as T1. **It would even be better if T2 is situated at a lower price than T1**. The appearance of T2 also meets the **first criterion in the 3MS principle** – failure to form a higher high in an uptrend. Bear in mind we still cannot confirm a complete formation of a double top until after T2 appears. Let's take a look at an unexpected scenario in which a potential double top fails to work with its original function.

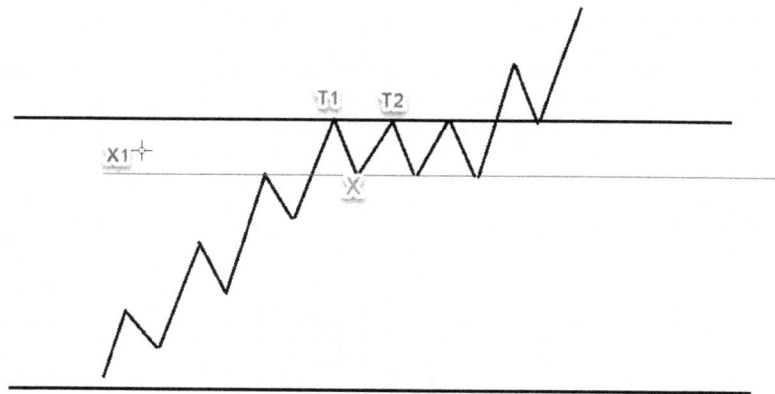

In this scenario, the appearance of T2 opens the first opportunity for sellers as buyers show signs of tiredness. However, the price cannot break the X1 line. Instead, it moves sideways between the upper resistance and the X1 line before breaking the resistance and continuing its uptrend. This is an unfavorable situation that may cost traders a lot of money because of their Fear Of Missing Out (FOMO – as you often hear in trading).

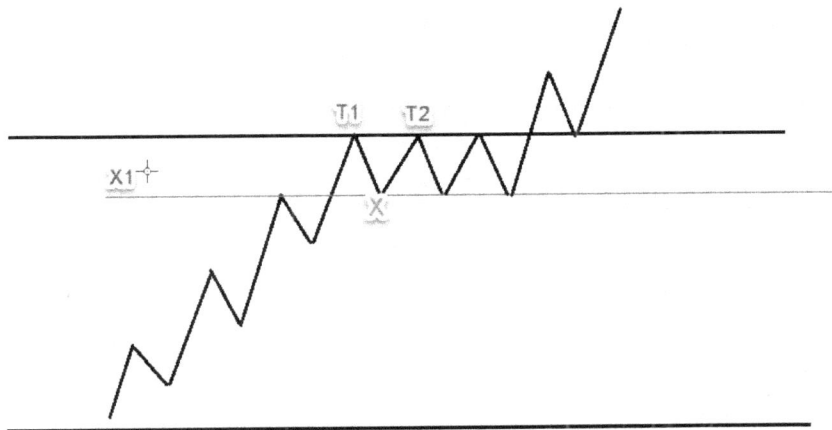

We can see the problem of this trading style from another angle. Remember what the characteristics of a downtrend movement are? Lower highs and lower lows.

Think about it. If you assume the uptrend has officially ended and a downtrend has been launched, problems may arise. The X could be seen as a low during a potential downtrend, however, we haven't witnessed any lower low, thus the downward signal here is not obvious. Put differently, the buyers are still having an advantage at this point. Simple as that.

Remember that trading obscure or unclear patterns is unlikely to benefit us in the long run. I have always tried to reinforce one principle in all my books: **Stay on the sideline** and **wait for other signals** when encountering unclear signals.

- Wait for the price to break the neckline

It is exactly what the **second condition in my 3MS principle** is about. In fact, a double top pattern is only confirmed after prices break the X1 line (the neckline). Take a look at the below picture.

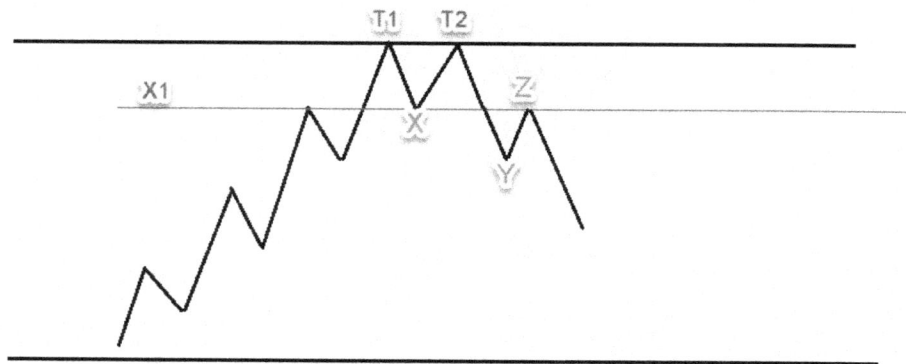

Yes, we've found it. Y is exactly what we are looking for. Once the price breaks the neckline and forms a lower low at Y, the double top pattern is "officially launched" and we just wait for one more retest at Z to enter a trade with a better chance of winning.

Note that there is one small variation on trading double top/bottom compared to the 3MS principle, where T2 can be at the same price level as T1, meaning that in the new downtrend, Z is the first lower high (instead of T2). However, even T2 is lower or at the same price as T1, it carries in itself a sign of rejection, preventing the price to continue its original trend.

- Double top/bottom in connection with 3MS principle

Now, let's dig a little bit deeper into market structure analysis in connection with the double top/bottom pattern. As we've learned, the three criteria for determining a reliable change in market structure (uptrend to downtrend) include:

- The market fails to create a higher high.
- The price breaks the last low in the previous uptrend.
- The market successfully creates two lower highs in the new downtrend, and the second high must not be higher than the last low in the previous uptrend.

Have you ever wondered why I emphasize the *failure to create a higher high* should *occur before* *the break of the last low in the previous uptrend*?

Simply put, this saves us from unexpected price fluctuations.

Take a look at a scenario where the price breaks the neckline before forming the second top.

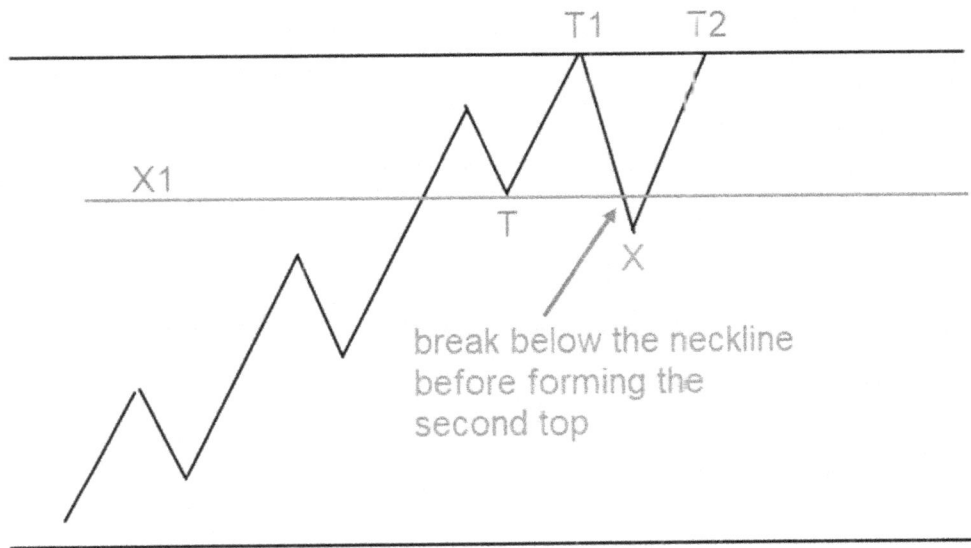

T1   T2

X1

T

X

break below the neckline
before forming the
second top

In this picture, the uptrend is strong until T1. While the price has yet to express any signs of failure to break the highest high (T1), it suddenly breaks the last low (T) in the initial uptrend.

The bears seem to outshine the bulls at this point. Starting from T1, which is positioned at a key resistance area, many traders may be confident in a reversal in the market. They try to pull the prices lower than the X1 line (drawn from the last low during the uptrend, parallel to the resistance level), forming a low at X. While it seems that a break below the X1 line paves the way for the formation of a downtrend, there are two potential dangers that traders need to take into consideration.

First, as I have mentioned, for a market structure to change from an uptrend to a downtrend, there should be enough conditions of **the 3MS principle**. Accordingly, this pattern fails to meet the third criterion. Hence, in this example, an "official" downtrend has not been launched. As the downtrend has not been confirmed, the chance of winning the trade is not as high as in the recommended scenario. From my experience, in an unpredictable environment, if method 2 produces a higher probability of success than method 1, stick to method 2.

Second, as we know from previous Chapters, in many cases, the market tends to come back to retest support/resistance. Thus, though the neckline has been broken, there might be an unexpected chance of the price coming back to the support/resistance. While we aren't sure how far the retest can go, it would be better to wait for other signals instead of entering a trade right after the breakout.

Below is a real example of reversal from a downtrend to an uptrend. The price broke the nearest high before forming a higher low in the emerging uptrend. This may not be considered a typical double bottom trading, but it gives us a perfect warning about how the price tends to remember the old key level, and that your stop-loss could be hit.

In this example, there was a clear downtrend until B. From there, the price easily broke the last high in the downtrend (A) and formed a new high at C. You can see how risky it was to enter a buy order without waiting for the market to form a higher low than B (the retest).

While things seemed not ideal when the market broke the last high right after the downtrend bottom, patience could help you in this case. With the presence of F as the retest on the X2 level, we now have two higher lows (D&F) and one higher high (E), the minimum condition for a possible uptrend. Entering the trade at F would yield a bigger probability of success now that the 3MS principle has been fully satisfied.

In the next section, we'll go into detail about how to set suitable order prices for your trade. But for now, let's take a look at my preferred double top scenario, where T2 is a little bit lower than T1. The principle is completely similar in double bottom trading when T2 is positioned a little higher than T1. You may get my idea on trading this ideal pattern, but we still talk more about it in a real example at the end of the chapter.

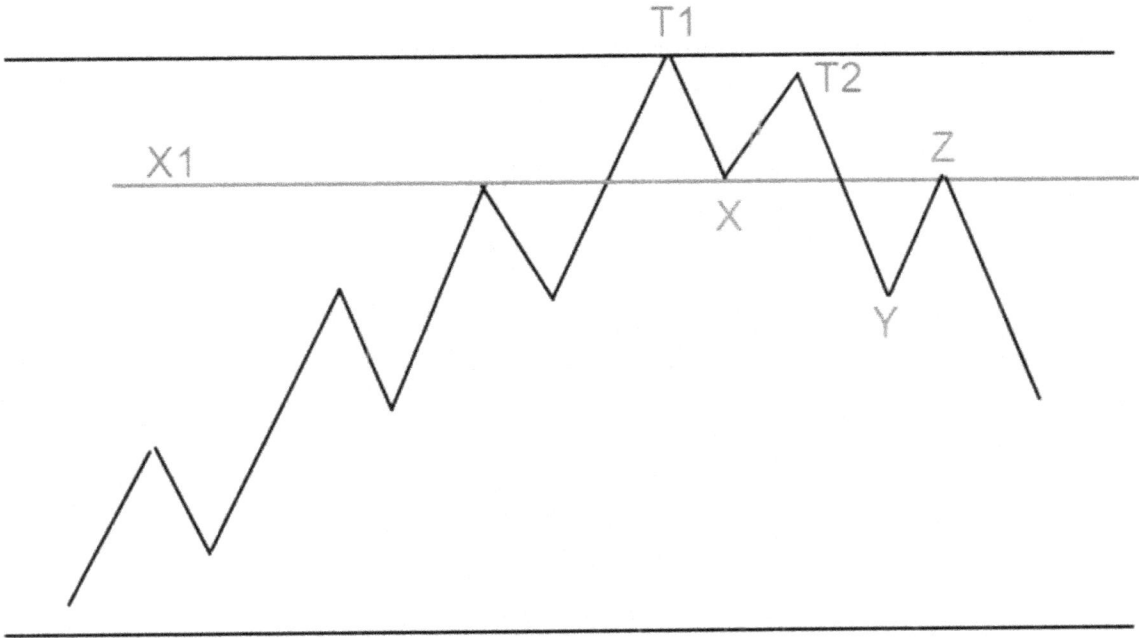

Honestly, I don't refute the fact that in some cases, the market would plummet without retesting the nearest support/resistance. Some risk-tolerant traders can still make some profits without waiting for the market to form an "official" downtrend (at least two lower highs after the top A). Once again, it depends on each trader's style in choosing the most compatible trading method. If you are a risk-averse trader, the 3MS principle could be an option worth trying.

2. How to trade double top/bottom

As can be seen from the picture below, the best trade entry should be placed around Z when the market retests the new resistance level (the X1 line). Meanwhile, a stop-loss should be placed just above the T2 and a profit-taking price should be targeted at the next support area. There will be more on stop-loss and profit-taking levels later, and this is how my strategy might be different from other books or courses.

- *Let's take a look at the entry point first.*

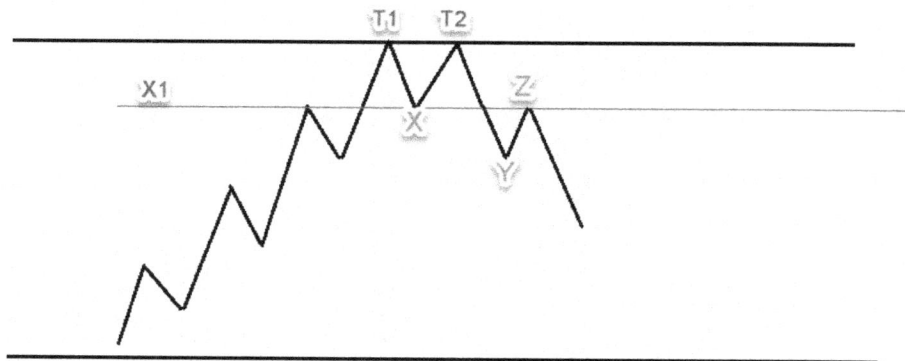

Some of you may ask: "Hey Frank, why not enter a sell order at T2, which seems to be the better price for sellers?"

My trading principle is to avoid doing things that are just a matter of luck. Trading at T2 might be an example of placing your trade on pure luck as sellers' pressure is not overwhelming the buying power. We don't deny that sometimes you can be right on trading at T2 and yielding some nice profit.

Yet, to me, it is more secure to enter your trade at Z when the 3MS principle has been confirmed. I will not guarantee that you will have a hundred percent win on trading at Z. Trading does not have anything to do with being right or wrong on any individual trade. It is more aligned with your long-term view. If you repeat the best possible actions with a large enough number of trades, you should find yourself gradually joining the "consistent profit group".

As I mentioned, finding an entry level in double bottom trading is very similar, where Z plays as the first higher low in the emerging uptrend.

- *How to set stop-loss and take-profit levels.*

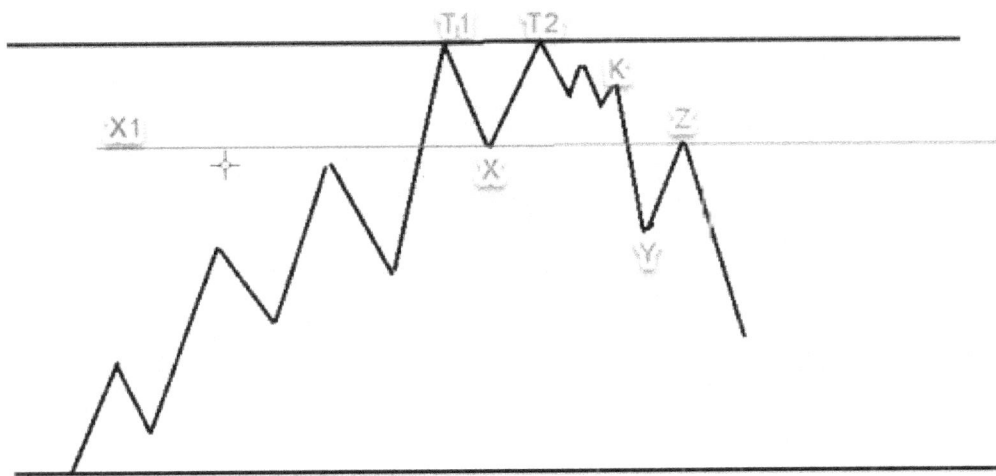

a. *Setting a stop-loss price*

While I strongly agree that you should apply the traditional use of stop-loss setting, i.e., a few pips above T2 (a safe/prudent stop loss level), I suggest you consider specific market movements and structures before deciding on your best possible stop-loss levels. The picture above could be seen as a typical example.

Before creating an obvious lower low at Y, the market displays certain hesitance from T2 to K. The seller's side is generally stronger than the buyers, though not distinct. From K, the market strongly breaks the key X1 line and confirms the formation of a double top pattern. If you have traded long enough, you may share with me the idea that on trading at Z, the stop loss is not necessarily placed above T2. Instead, placement of stop loss just above K could still save you from unexpected losses while bringing a better risk/reward ratio. Notice how the market constantly creates minor lower highs and lower lows from T2 to K, signaling that the sellers are gaining more and more strength. While increasing your risk/reward ratio, a stop loss above K would not be likely to deprive you of opportunities in case of a rally above the K level.

Things are similar in double bottom trading where a stop-loss below T2 or below K could be considered, depending on each specific circumstance.

b. *Where to take profit?*

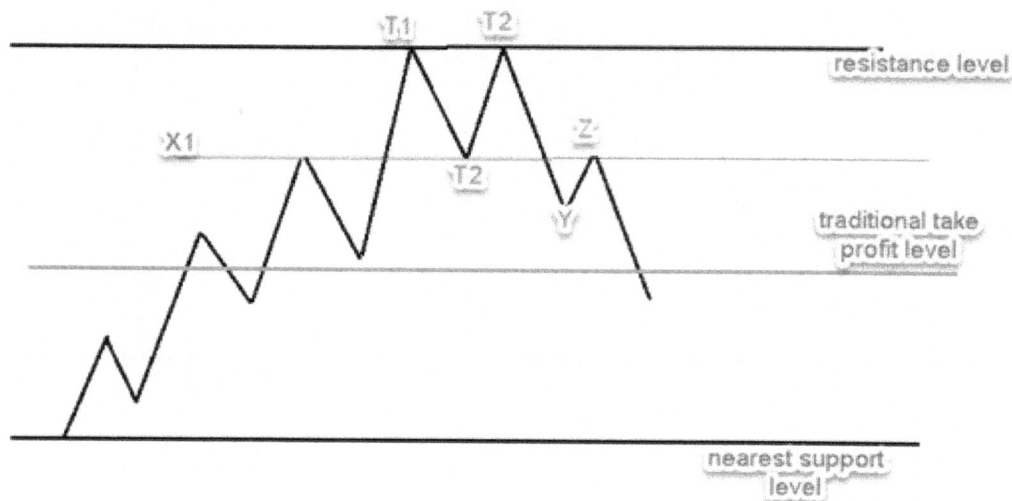

If you have read some books on the double top pattern, a recommended profit level would be equal to the distance from the entry point (the neckline) to the top, i.e., the 1:1 ratio. This is a safe profit level in my opinion, yet the risk/reward ratio is not so impressive in trading. To maximize your trade efficiency, I wouldn't recommend the 1:1 ratio. It is fixed, and is not a "long-term profitable ratio". In the following chapter, you will see how a good risk/reward ratio would make your trading journey much more comfortable than you can ever expect, and is an indispensable part of any successful trading method.

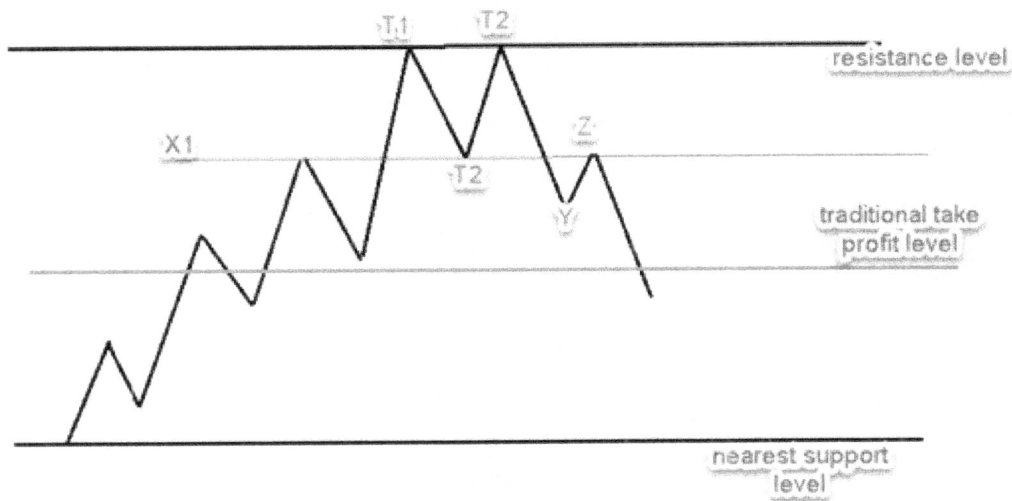

From my experience, a possible profit-taking level in trading double top is the nearest (key) support level. It is where there is a higher chance of a fluctuation in price. While we cannot tell within certainty whether there will be a reversal at any key level, it would never be a bad idea to stack part or the whole profit and wait for other price actions before deciding the next steps.

Regarding double bottom trading, the next resistance is when traders may consider closing their trading positions partly or entirely.

Now, let's take a look at some real examples of trading double top/bottom.

GBP/CAD
Daily chart

neckline

retest - entry price

double bottom

1.77000
1.76172
1.75000
1.74000
1.73000
1.71777
1.71000
1.70663
1.69963
1.69000
1.67952
1.67100
1.66200

May   Jun   Jul

In this chart, the market was in a clear downtrend before forming a double bottom pattern at a key level. Those two bottoms are at the same price level. After the second bottom, the price made a strong rally, breaking the neckline, signaling a possible uptrend. Notice how the price made an ideal retest to the neckline soon after breaking it, creating a perfect trade opportunity for an entry.

With a stop-loss placed just below the bottoms and the profit-taking levels at around the next resistance zone (1.7617), here is what happened next regarding the pair:

GBP/CAD
Daily chart

Price levels
1.77000
1.76172
1.75000
1.74686
1.74000
1.73000
1.72000
1.71777
1.71000
1.69963
1.69000
1.67952
1.67000
1.66100

profit-target is easily hit with an ideal R/R of 1:3

entry price

stop-loss

May   Jun   Jul   Aug

This is a perfect example of why choosing the next resistance might bring a better profit (R/R of 1:3) compared to the fixed 1:1 ratio. From the retest, the price shot up to the target without any opposing force from the bears. Now, if the next resistance is too far from the entry price, should we aim to close the whole position at that price?

The answer is that it depends on many factors. What is your trading style? How risk-tolerant are you? Are you using some other tools for trailing stop-loss? What is your trading timeframe? And so on.

It's hard to give a black and white answer here. One of my favorite methods is the one that we've already heard about: View the chart in a shorter timeframe. Doing this, you may find different key levels to consider closing parts of your position gradually. One thing I can assure you is the obvious benefits of closing the trades at a key level compared to a fixed ratio (for example 1:1).

Now, let's move to an example regarding the double top pattern trading.

second top is a little lower than the first

neckline

GBP/CHF
Daily chart

1.38094
1.37000
1.36224
1.36177
1.35000
1.34000
1.33000
1.32000
1.31087
1.30400
1.29600
1.28800

15   Mar   19   Apr   16   May

This is the perfect example that I mentioned above, where the second top is just a little bit lower than the first top during the double top formation.

The market was in a very smooth uptrend until X, which played like a higher low, or a correction during the process. From that, buyers tried to take the price to the resistance level, forming a double top pattern. However, the bears jumped in very quickly, taking the price back below the neckline.

The message of a lower price in the second top lies mainly in the momentum of the market. In many financial markets, retests are common. In this case, failing to make a "perfect" retest at the key resistance level, especially with the presence of a long bearish candlestick, indicates the upward momentum was endangered. This is when we should be prepared for other precious trade signals.

A seemingly imperfect double top turned out to be a perfect illustration of a break in the market structure, creating two lower highs at Y and Y' (the retest), and one lower low at Z. This is the minimum condition for a downtrend to form, and now we have it.

As long as the retest at Y' doesn't violate the territory above the neckline, entering the trade around Y might bring you a nice profit in many cases. As you can see in the picture below, the price plummeted after revisiting the neckline.

From my personal experience, a double top/bottom pattern may not appear as frequently as engulfing or pin bar candlesticks. Yet, once it is present, some nice profits might await you. Once again, whether or not you can use the pattern effectively depends on how you understand the message via candlesticks and the correlation among them.

The three patterns in this book – engulfing pattern, pin bar, and double top/bottom -- are considered the most popular and powerful ones in financial trading. With some practice, you can be confident in identifying the true opportunities in highly volatile and unpredictable financial markets.

In the next chapter, I will answer one of the most common yet difficult questions regarding the art of management in trading.

CHAPTER X: SEVEN-STEP SUCCESS FORMULA IN TRADING

We've learned some powerful trading methods with deep analyses of the market momentum and candlestick patterns. While the methods themselves play an important part in driving a trader's course of action, successful trading requires more from participants. This section is about seven mind-blowing secrets in keeping and growing money in the financial markets.

Every trader participating in financial trading aims to make decent money from it. However, before thinking of profiting from the market, traders must strive to save their trading account at all costs. Regrettably, most of them fail to protect their hard-earned capital for many different reasons. Below are some of the most common pitfalls that can cause trading accounts to be ruined.

1. Reasons for accounts to be ruined

- *Poor capital management*

Capital management is the most crucial factor that differentiates a seasoned trader from an amateur trader.

Just like dieting and exercising, capital management does not seem to be a pleasant way to spend your time. Good capital management entails closely monitoring positions so traders can always make sure to keep their trading under control. One of the most important yet overlooked aspects of trading is loss-taking. Poor management and loss-taking strategies can lead to a much bigger burden to traders. Look at the table below:

Amount Of Equity Lost	Amount Of Return Necessary To Restore To Original Equity Value
25%	33%
50%	100%

75%	400%
90%	1000%

Many traders often pursue potential profits without being aware of the dangers of losses when their expectations turn out to be wrong. As can be seen from the table above, a trader would have to earn 100% on his/her capital just to bring it back to the original equity value. When the drawdown is 75%, the trader must quadruple his/her trading account just to break even – a Herculean task.

The more they lose, the more traders strive to get back what they used to have. More often than not, traders tend to open new positions where the signals are not very clear, or in some other cases, just by following others' trade ideas. The more they "try", the more likely their trading account can be blown away. It all boils down to poor capital management.

- ### *Poor emotion management*

Emotion management plays a huge part in determining whether a trader can be successful long-term. You may have heard that psychology control accounts for 70% of success in the financial market. Yet, very few people can control their trades in an appropriate way, and let negative emotions take over their decision-making process. Below are six major negative emotions in trading that can have a damaging impact on your trading results.

- Fear

Fear is probably the most frequently discussed topic in trading psychology. It can be seen in a number of cases that can cause trading mistakes. For example, when the trade goes against your expectations, the fear of losing money dominates, preventing you from cutting the necessary losses, just to endure a bigger loss eventually. On the contrary, when a trade goes favorably, the fear of losing your money causes you to close the trade too early instead of letting profits run.

- Greed

While greed may help you to find good opportunities in some ways, it can be detrimental to your trading account. Driven by greed, traders may forget about risk management principles in pursuit of profit. Greed paves the way for a gambling mindset, where impulsive decisions start to take control over your trading activities.

- Hope

Hope is believed to be positive in many cases. However, in trading, hope can have a bad impact on your trading account. In a losing position, for example, a ray of hope can delay your cutting-loss action, causing the loss to become bigger, even to the extent your account can be swept away. On another angle, hope can lead to unrealistic expectations, causing you to open a bigger position and taking your account to a dangerous level.

- Anxiety

If you feel uncomfortable with your trade, there might be something wrong with your trading decision. This feeling can result from failure to analyze the trade setup and triggers carefully, or the fact that you open the trade with a bigger size than you should.

Hence, it's better to keep track of your expectations and excitement carefully. Failing to keep a balanced state of mind might be the signal that you should temporarily avoid trading.

- Frustration

Frustration is among the worst psychological traits in trading. When you encounter losses after losses or close a trade in a loss (or a small profit) instead of a decent profit, frustration can easily take over your mind. It can reinforce other negative feelings and lead to more unwise trading decisions (such as opening consecutive impulsive trades). This is one of the easiest ways to take your account balance to zero.

- ***Failure to build an appropriate trading strategy***

A trading strategy is mostly about the way you analyze the market and how you utilize that analysis to pinpoint the best opportunities in the market and make money from them. Yet, many traders struggle with finding an appropriate strategy for their trading journey. They switch from one strategy to another constantly without improving their trading results. Losses after losses occur, and this, in turn, becomes an ideal situation for negative emotions to emerge, and then the final result… we all know.

Below are some signs of an inappropriate trading strategy:

- *It's hard to follow*

If your trading strategy is too unclear, too complicated, or takes too much of your time, it may be an indication of a bad approach that doesn't suit you. You might choose to make necessary adjustments to the strategy or switch to another strategy completely.

- *The trading system is too weak*

This might be surprising, but some traders stick to a one-indicator strategy without any effort to optimize it. While there is nothing wrong with using only one indicator in your trading system, finding a "more complex" system that works well across different assets and timeframes might be a better option. In previous books, I emphasize the use of **confirmation signals**, in which a trade won't be executed unless there are at least two indicators or tools approving the trade signal.

- *Your trades are mostly unsuccessful*

This is obvious. If you consistently experience losses, or if your loss rate is too high after you have used in different markets, there might be something wrong with your trading approach. I won't say that establishing a high win rate strategy is a "must". I just want to emphasize the need to optimize your trading strategy, where necessary, so that it can produce better results and long-term overall profits.

2. How can we avoid market traps and make consistent profits?

There are not many guarantees I can make to you as a trader. But there is one guarantee I can confidently make here: If you consistently follow the techniques in executing your trade presented below, the chance of blowing up your trading account is next to zero.

Trading success includes three main elements: a good trading system, good capital management, and good psychology management.

Most traders focus too much on profit in the trading endeavor. It seems not to be a problem at first because profit is what drives traders to the trading journey. But it is truly a problem, a BIG problem. When a trader focuses solely on profits, he only expects winning trades because they bring him profits. He somewhat ignores the losing ones, or in other words, is afraid of losing trades because they push him away from his target. If you understand that losing trades, even a lot of losing trades, are indispensable in trading, you can feel how dangerous it is when you ignore or are afraid of them. This is when you are not aligning your mindset correctly. To many of my students, I always emphasize one big lesson when joining the market: Don't think about profits at the beginning of the trading journey. Think about how to protect your account, first and foremost.

Now comes the **7-step success formula** in trading. Again, this is among the very few things I can guarantee and **if you apply these consistently, your account will be safe for a long time.**

- Find an appropriate trading strategy.
- Verify its effectiveness by doing back-testing.
- Open a trading account with an appropriate provider (To me, it's an account with a low spread – bid/ask difference).
- Use the daily chart for your trading decision.
- Risk per trade: 1% - 1.5% (highly recommended 1% for newbies).
- Set a risk/reward ratio: at least 1:2.5 (ideally 1:3 or better).
- Set a trade frequency: maximum of 10 per month.

Most of the above elements have become familiar with you as a trader, except the back-testing process. Hence, before diving into how the 7-step formula can change your trading career, let's talk about back-testing first.

Back-testing is, in my opinion, the most underrated weapon in trading and investing. It is the process of looking back at historical data and applying your strategy to dozens or hundreds of opportunities to see how it performs. The underlying theory is that a strategy that performed well in the past tends to work well in the future, and vice versa.

Back-testing gives a more objective view over many different market conditions. Moreover, back-testing gives you the chance to make necessary adjustments to better optimize your strategy.

Back-testing is not glamorous or pleasant. Sometimes, it is considered boring, difficult, or even pointless (by amateur traders). However, every trading mentor and professional would highly recommend you back-test all strategies you intend to use in order to find a trade entry, stop-loss, and profit-taking level.

Back-testing can be done automatically via some paid tools or manually. While I don't object to the use of fancy tools, manual back-testing has always fascinated me more. The underlying reason is simple: *I always want to put myself in a position as if I were doing a real trade.* Doing this, we could learn how to resist the temptation of opening a trade in many cases, how to manage our emotions after successive losses or wins, how to twist our strategy in some different circumstances, and much more. All these advantages come from the fact that we are constantly in front of each candlestick movement. Systematic back-testing would not be able to bring us such precious experience.

With the development of many trading platforms, we can easily get access to free back-testing tools instead of investing hundreds or even thousands of dollars for fancy software. One of the most user-friendly platforms for back-testing the reliability of any strategy is tradingview.com. All you need to do is to click at the *bar replay* symbol on the menu and choose a starting point for the replay. Or, if you need a tutorial, visit https://bit.ly/327AXVN for a detailed video guiding you through how to back-test a trading strategy on this platform.

Back-testing without a detailed record of how your strategy performs would be of little use. A spreadsheet which records all relevant information in connection with your strategy's performance over past price behaviors is highly recommended.

Now that you've discovered the importance of back-testing, below is the magic resulting from the application of the 7-step formula that can take your trading to the next level:

1. Patience

The timeframe used: If you've just stepped into trading, trading on the daily timeframe may be a serious challenge that undermines most participants. The mere transition from a shorter chart (i.e the 5 minute or 30 minute one) to the daily chart can require huge perseverance, discipline, and patience. You won't have the chance to open trade after trade like before because it takes one day for a candlestick to finish and several candlesticks to find a trade setup. It's hard to stick to the daily chart, but it's truly worth it. You will feel how patient you are after a period.

Risk/reward ratio: Trade setups may not be very hard to spot on a trading chart, but an ideal trade setup with a favorable risk/reward of at least 1:2.5 is not easy to pick. This strengthens your concentration and patience as you look only for potential trade setups and triggers in the chart.

Maximum of 10 trades per month: It is hard to feel but whenever a trade is completed, whether it is a losing or winning trade, your emotion can be affected. Many traders I know execute dozens or even hundreds of trades per month, causing emotional chaos and the inability to concentrate on the trading rules and guidelines. In contrast, by limiting your maximum number of trades to only 10, you not only enhance your patience but also help keep a balanced state of mind.

2. Better capital management

Everyone knows the importance of capital management. By "know", I mean each trader hears about or reads about this at some time during his or her trading career. More importantly, traders generally agree that money management is critical to your trading success.

However, very few people can apply money management methods consistently in trading. In other words, it seems easy at first, where they reap some nice bucks in the market. However, when some losing trades appear, things change drastically. They shift their focus from protecting their accounts to getting back what has been lost at all costs, resulting in exceeding position size or arbitrary risk options.

Good capital management includes some important elements. One of the most important is the risk percentage per trade. As I stated above, never risk more than 1.5% per trade, or if you are a newbie, a risk level of 1% for each trade is recommended.

Suppose you apply the 1% risk percentage for each of your trades. In the worst case, you execute 10 trades in one month and all of them are losing ones, you only lose 10% of your trading account. Honestly, if you carefully find a trading strategy that suits your trading style and back-test it with a lot of trades using historical data, the chance of losing all 10 trades is very small.

Moreover, when applying the 1:3 risk/reward ratio, for example, for each winning trade, you are **allowed** to lose up to three other trades without reducing your equity balance. By applying this consistently, your account will be well protected for a long time. The biggest concern lies in how long you can stick to the formula. Most traders are vulnerable to breaking the rules after some time for different reasons.

3. Long-term success

As I mentioned, the big advantage of applying the 1:3 risk/reward ratio is that for each dollar you may lose in a trade, the potential profit is three times bigger. Hence, you don't need a high win rate to make long-term profits in the financial market (although it is what we all desire). Assume that you are applying the 1% risk management method in connection with the ideal risk/reward ratio (1:3), the table below shows the potential for your account to grow after the 7-step formula is applied consistently.

Winning trades (WT)	Losing trades (LT)	Overall equity changes (= WT*3% - LT*1%)
0	10	-10%
1	9	-6%
2	8	-2%
3	7	+2%
4	6	+6%
5	5	+10%
6	4	+14%
7	3	+18%
8	2	+22%
9	1	+26%
10	0	+30%
Average		10%

Do you see the magic?

There are 11 different scenarios that can occur to your trading account in a one-month period. Out of the maximum of ten trades taken, you just need to win three times to make profits. In other words, any time you make three winning trades in any month, you can be confident that you will **make profits** that month, even if the month just started. Can you see a more comfortable trading scenario than this?

Moreover, the average monthly equity change when applying this formula is +10% - a spectacular profit margin if you are aware that more than 90 percent of traders lose money in financial trading.

To sum up, the 7-step formula is a short, concise, and effective summary of how you should perform in the financial market. Most trading courses and books may show a lot of ingredients that must be included in your trading endeavor, to an extent that you will find it hard to build a complete trading system. Via this system, I truly hope it can give you a good idea of what to look for and how to protect and grow your trading account in one of the most challenging endeavors ever.

www.ingramcontent.com/pod-product-compliance
Lightning Source LLC
Chambersburg PA
CBHW081746200326
41597CB00024B/4405